The Holyday Book

FRANCIS X. WEISER

The Holyday Book

ILLUSTRATED BY ROBERT FRANKENBERG

ST. AUGUSTINE ACADEMY PRESS
HOMER GLEN, ILLINOIS

This edition reprinted in 2018
by St. Augustine Academy Press

ISBN: 978-1-64051-056-2

Proceeds from the sale of this book will be donated to a fund for the support of Seminarians studying for the priesthood.

IMPRIMI POTEST: William E. FitzGerald, S.J., Provincial
NIHIL OBSTAT: Michael P. Noonan, S.M., S.T.D., Diocesan Censor
IMPRIMATUR: ✠ Richard J. Cushing, D.D., Archbishop of Boston
DATE: March 17, 1956

ACKNOWLEDGMENTS: To Polanie Publishing Co., Minneapolis, Minn., for permission to reprint a recipe. To Edward C. Currie for his assistance in research on music. To Rev. Claude Klarkowski for providing and translating Polish texts. Also to the Sisters of Colegio San José, San Germán, Puerto Rico, Sister Marie Marguerite, S.N.D., Rev. Gregory Tom, Rev. Robert E. Maloney, S.J., Miss Helen Landreth, and Miss Margaret O'Loughlin.

The notes referred to by number throughout the text are to be found at the end of the book.

Figures in parentheses after the names of persons indicate the year of death.

TO THE LITURGICAL MOVEMENT
IN THE UNITED STATES

Foreword

"Many people celebrate the holydays and know their names; but of their history, meaning and origin they know nothing. . . . Truly, such ignorance deserves to be blamed and ridiculed."

Almost sixteen hundred years ago Saint John Chrysostom, the great Patriarch of Constantinople, thundered these words from the pulpit at the immense crowd of people gathered to hear his sermon. Like so many others of Chrysostom's words they ring eternally true, for he was not only a masterful orator but also knew human nature in all its weakness and strength.

Perhaps the people of his time could have answered the Saint as many a listener would answer today: "How can I know the meaning and history of the feasts, 'unless someone shows me' [Acts 8, 31]?"

This book was written to provide the information which Saint John Chrysostom would have wished the faithful to possess. However, so rich in number, variety, and meaning are the liturgical and extraliturgical celebrations of the festive seasons, as well as of the individual feasts, that it seemed appropriate to gather their significant details in separate volumes. The seasons of Christmas and Easter (with Lent) I treated previously in *The Christmas Book* (1952) and *The Easter Book* (1954). This volume is devoted to the season of Pentecost and to those feasts of saints throughout the year that have attained the rank of holydays or popular festivals in the course of centuries.

Classified within the vast field of knowledge, these three books form a compendium of heortology, a historical science which explains the origin, development, and meaning of feasts. The word is derived from the Greek *heorte* (feast) and *logos* (discourse).

It is the author's wish that this final book of the trilogy, which completes the cycle of the Year of the Lord, may not only deepen the understanding of our feasts but also inspire a more fruitful and joyful celebration in church, home, and heart.

FRANCIS X. WEISER, S.J.

Weston College
Weston, Massachusetts

Contents

Notes on Chapter Illustrations

11

The Year of the Lord

Christ Himself introduced the very first liturgical celebration when, at the Last Supper, He bade the Apostles re-enact the mysteries of the Redemption (1 Cor.
11, 23-26). Ever since that night the performance of the
"sacred mysteries" (meaning, in this connection, the
Holy Sacrifice) has remained the very center and soul
of all Christian liturgy. What developed in the hearts
and minds of men was merely the accidental form and
frame which the liturgical action assumed in the course
of time.

Feasts of the Lord · The liturgical celebrations form
an organic unit which consists of the three festivals and
seasons of Christmas (with Advent), Easter (with

13

Lent), and Pentecost (with the rest of the year).
Around the principal act of the sacrifice of the Mass
these feasts have gradually developed a rich and inspiring ceremonial of liturgical rites, each expressing
the particular significance of the feast and making it a
part of the spiritual needs of the faithful who devoutly
attend the festive service.

From early times, too, the radiation of sacred thought
and action in the liturgical service inspired the people
to introduce the spirit and meaning of each feast into
their own lives and homes. It was in this way that the
many popular customs and traditions connected with
the feasts came into existence in all Christian countries. Most of the symbols and customs are imitations
of ecclesiastical rites and expressions of liturgical
thought. In the course of centuries, however, their origin and true significance has been forgotten in many
places.

Sundays · From the time of the Apostles, Sunday has
been the day on which the official worship of God takes
place in the form of the Eucharistic Sacrifice (Acts 20,
7). After the cessation of the persecutions in 313, the
Sunday service was transferred from the secrecy of
the catacombs to the serene and solemn halls of the
basilicas (court buildings) which Emperor Constantine
(337) gave to the early Christians as places of public
worship.

As the day of Christ's Resurrection and the weekly

holyday of the Christian era, Sunday also became the new "Day of the Lord," the center of the liturgical week, on which the faithful attended the sacred mysteries in church. It became, and remained, a day of rest and prayer, of deep spiritual joy, the memorial day of Christ's Resurrection, a "little Easter." Fasting and penitential services are excluded on Sundays, and the faithful observe the day by resting from their usual occupations. Civic legislation, too, has acknowledged Sunday as the general day of rest and religious character in most countries of the civilized world. (See Chapter 2.)

Feasts of Mary · A great and popular veneration of Mary, the Mother of God (*Theotokos*), existed in the early Church long before any special feast was instituted in her honor. To her is accorded a veneration (*hyperdulia*) that transcends the honor given to any other saint (*dulia*).[1] Her dignity as the Mother of the Incarnate Word of God, and the spiritual privileges conferred on her by reason of this dignity, raise her beyond all created spirits to the exalted position of "Queen of all Saints." On the other hand, she still remains a mere creature in all her glory. The Church has never "adored" Mary or accorded her any honors that are reserved for Divinity.

Wall paintings in the Roman catacombs, dating from the first half of the second century, picture her holding the Divine Child, usually with a Biblical scene for

15

background. The earliest apocrypha (legendary Christion literature) of the second century bear eloquent testimony to the veneration that was accorded Mary at the very dawn of Church history. The first known hymns and poetical prayers to her were written by the deacon of the church of Ephesus, Saint Ephrem the Syrian (373). His twenty *madrase* (poems) on Mary breathe not only tender devotion but classic beauty as well. Here is a translation of a stanza of one of his hymns:

> Blessed are you, Mary, for in your soul dwelled the
> 	Holy Spirit of Whom David sang.
> Blessed are you who were deemed worthy to be greeted
> 	by the Father through Gabriel's mouth.
> Blessed are you who were made to be the living chariot
> 	of the Son of God.
>
> 	He stood on your knees,
> 	He lay in your arms,
> He drank from the fountains of your breasts.
> He rested, a baby, in your embrace:
> But His gown was the flaming light of Divinity.[2]

The feasts of our Lady observed in the universal Church are quite numerous. They form a radiant pattern of festive commemorations through the year. Some of them have affected the public life of communities and countries for many centuries. Others are celebrated only within the confines of liturgical service. All of them cast the light and warmth of their blessing into the hearts of devout Christians everywhere.

Five festivals, called the "major feasts of Mary," were kept as public holydays (and holidays) up to the present century. It was as recently as 1918 that the new Code of Canon Law dropped three of them from the list of prescribed holydays. In the liturgy, however, they still retain their place, and rank as major feasts. Many ancient customs connected with them have survived to our day.

Feasts of Saints · Interwoven with the festive seasons and the cycles of weekly liturgy is the liturgical system of saints' days. From the beginnings of Christianity there has been no doubt (as there was none among the Jews) that persons who led a life of great holiness or suffered and died for the cause of God enjoyed the glories of a special reward in Heaven and deserved highest esteem and veneration from the faithful on earth. The Bible itself has preserved the memory of such heroes of God as the patriarchs, prophets, holy kings, Machabees, and many others, and of those who died for Christ—for example, the martyred children of Bethlehem, John the Baptist, Saint James the Great, and Saint Stephen.

In addition to these Biblical saints, Christians immediately began to honor the memory of those who died in the persecutions. This was done on a local scale within each Christian community. The tombs of the martyrs were held in high veneration. On the anniversary of their deaths Mass was celebrated over their graves and a sermon preached. Thus it happened, for instance, that Saint Pionius and his companions were seized by Roman soldiers while conducting the anniversary service at the tomb of Saint Polycarp of Smyrna (Asia Minor) in 250 and were themselves put to death and became martyrs of Christ.

In the Western Church, the conversion of the Germanic races brought about an extension of the local calendars of saints. Having no Christian past of their own, they adopted the ritual books of the Roman Church and her list of saints as well. It was not long, however, before they added the names of their own national heroes of God to the annual calendar of saints' feasts and thus prepared the way for a more universal calendar. In the course of the succeeding centuries the Roman list of saints' days was gradually widened by the authorities of the Church; it came to include saints of other local churches and other nations, until the Roman Missal and martyrology became truly representative of the universal Church.

In the Mass text, however, a relic of the original practice remains, for all saints mentioned in the Canon of the Mass (besides those of the Bible) are taken from the ancient list of the Italian community.[3] The Oriental Rites were even slower than Rome in adopting the feasts of "foreign" martyrs and saints. Up

THE YEAR OF THE LORD

to this day but few saints of the Western Church are celebrated in the East.

Festivals and Folklore · A great many of our modern customs and traditions connected with the feasts of the year have been inspired by liturgical thought and symbols. Thus, for instance, the Christmas tree originated in western Germany in the sixteenth century as a combination of the ancient "Paradise tree" of the mystery plays (a fir tree hung with apples) and of the candles (representing Christ as the Light of the World) plus the decorations (glass balls, tinsel, star of Bethlehem) of the traditional wooden "Christmas pyramid" as it was used in those parts of Germany.[4]

Another large group of popular traditions widely used is of pre-Christian origin. Very often these customs are said to be based on pagan practices. Actually, most of them were never connected with the worship of pagan gods, but were simply a part of the general nature lore and nature symbolism of the Indo-European races. A Yule tree, for instance, symbolized the fact that nature did not die under the ice and snow of winter, and that spring would come again. The little evergreen tree in the home was a token and symbol of this consoling certainty. It presented something beautifully and bravely alive while the rest of nature seemed to be dead. There is no direct religious connotation, pagan or Christian, in this custom—no more than in our modern practice of putting a flowerpot on the window sill.

Such ancient nature customs and symbols, which in themselves were not of pagan religious significance, were not only retained by the European nations after their conversion to Christianity but fitted charmingly into the pattern of their popular celebrations of the great feasts and seasons of the year. For instance, there is the custom today of putting up fir trees (without any decorations) in halls and even in churches at Christmas time. These fir trees, of course, are not Christmas trees; but they are used at Christmas to make our homes and halls and churches look more cheerful than at other times. They—and not the decorated Christmas tree—are the true descendants of the ancient Yule trees.

Many of these pre-Christian nature customs received a new significance through a symbolic or legendary connection with the events of a feast, like the Easter egg, an ancient symbol of fertility and new life, which was interpreted in Christian times as a symbol of the rock tomb out of which Christ gloriously emerged at His Resurrection. Another example is the ancient fertility custom of sprinkling water on people. This custom is now practiced in some countries at Easter time as a symbol of conferring on girls the blessings of the feast—protection from danger and sickness, a happy marriage, and fruitful motherhood.[5]

Finally, there is a large group of traditions usually

designated as "popular superstitions." It must be pointed out that there are two, basically different, kinds of beliefs that we commonly call "superstitions." The first attributes preternatural powers to a thing in itself without relation to God; for instance, the "power" of a rabbit's foot to protect from harm. This is obviously wrong. The second kind, often called "pious superstitions," does not ascribe preternatural powers to an object in itself but considers these powers as granted by God. An example is the belief that all running water is blessed with healing powers on Easter Sunday in honor of our Lord's Resurrection. Such a "pious superstition" is, of course, not wrong in itself, but it is erroneous, since there is no basis in Divine Revelation or in ecclesiastical authority for such a belief.

Liturgy and Legend · Many feasts of the year, especially those of the early saints, are connected with traditional observances based on mere legendary claims. Hence it might seem to the less-informed reader that the popular veneration of the saints is but a sentimental tribute originating from unhistorical, and sometimes ridiculous, legendary beliefs.

Actually, these traditional observances rest on the bedrock of liturgical piety which has always remained the source of popular celebration. Every true Christian knows from childhood that the basis of his devotion to the saints is not some fictional event or legendary patronage (although he might celebrate them, too), but the very real and historical fact of the saints' heroic service to God and love of men, the radiant perfection of their lives in Christian virtue and faith.

The liturgical prayers hardly ever mention any of the legendary elements with which popular tradition abounds, but quote the historical facts of martyrdom or heroic virtue and perfect faith. It was on this basis only that the Church tolerated those additional expressions of legendary observance outside the liturgy. The liturgical Mass prayers of the various feasts, which may be found at the end of chapters in this book, will serve as illustration and proof.

Holydays of Obligation · According to the new Code of Canon Law (1918), the religious obligation of keeping a holyday (attendance at Mass and rest from servile work) extends to all Sundays of the year, and to ten other feasts—Circumcision (New Year's Day), Epiphany, Saint Joseph's Day, Ascension Thursday, Corpus Christi, Peter and Paul's Day, Assumption of Mary, All Saints' Day, Immaculate Conception, Christmas Day (Can. 1247).

In the United States, however, four of these feasts (Epiphany, Saint Joseph's, Corpus Christi, Peter and Paul's) are exempt from the obligation by dispensation of the Holy See. On the prescribed feasts which fall on weekdays and are not legal holidays (Ascension, Assumption, All Saints, Immaculate Conception), the faithful are obliged to attend Mass but are dispensed from the law of holyday rest.

Pentecost Season

CHAPTER 1

The Sundays

The system of dividing the moon month (twenty-eight days) into four parts and of keeping a day of rest in each period of seven days is of very ancient origin. At the time of Abraham it was generally observed among the Hebrews and other nations of the East. The Bible reports the creation as taking place within six days; and the subsequent "resting" of the Lord on the seventh day reveals the Sabbath as instituted and sanctified by God (Gen. 2, 3). Consequently, the Sabbath rest was enjoined by the Law of Moses under severe sanctions. The daily labor for providing the necessities of life was to be laid aside. Neither travel nor business transactions were allowed, and no work could be done in farm or garden or house. Even the food for the Sabbath meals had to be prepared on the preceding day. For this reason Friday came to be called *paraskeve* (Day of Preparation).

More important, however, than the Sabbath rest (which the Pharisees exaggerated by their gratuitous restrictions) was the duty of worship. The official daily sacrifice in the Temple was doubled on the Sabbath, additional prayers were prescribed, and the people who lived outside Jerusalem attended the synagogues (meeting houses) for religious instruction and common prayer.

In the New Testament there is no evidence that Christ or the Apostles immediately abolished the Sabbath. In fact, the Apostles for some years observed it along with other practices of the Old Testament (see Acts 18, 4). At the same time they celebrated Sunday as the new Christian day of worship because it was the day of Christ's Resurrection (Acts 20, 7). Saint Paul declared that the keeping of the Sabbath was not binding on the Gentile Christians (Col. 2, 16). It seems, however, that the converts from Judaism continued to observe the Sabbath for quite some time. This custom prompted various local churches of the Orient to keep both Saturday and Sunday as holydays, until the Council of Laodicaea in the fourth century forbade this double observance.[6] The Greek Church preserves a special distinction for Saturday to the present: like Sunday, it is always exempt from the law of fast or abstinence.

The name of Sunday, in Jewish reckoning, was "the first day after the Sabbath" (*prima Sabbati*). It is so designated in the Gospel reports of the Resurrection (Matt. 28, 1). Very soon the early Christians named it the "Day of the Lord" (*Kyriake, Dominica*) as may be seen in the Apocalypse of Saint John (1, 10). According to official Roman usage the day was called Sun Day (*Dies Solis*), for the Romans had accepted the Egyptian custom of naming the seven days of the week after the sun, the moon, and the gods of the planets. Later, during the migrations, the Germanic nations substituted their own gods for those of the Romans, and thus came about our modern names of the weekdays: Sunday (sun), Monday (moon), Tuesday (Thiu), Wednesday (Woden), Thursday (Thor), Friday (Frija). Only Saturday retained its Roman name (Day of Saturn).

The early Christians in the Roman Empire used both the apostolic name (Day of the Lord) and the popular term (Sun Day). The Latin nations kept the form "Day of the Lord" (*Dominica* in Italian and Portuguese, *Dimanche* in French, *Domingo* in Spanish, *Domineca* in Rumanian). The other form, "Day of the Sun," is used by the Germanic and Slavic nations (*Sunday* in English, *Sonntag* in German, *Sondag* in Scandinavian, *Nedelja* in Slavonic).

The Greek Church and its people still use the ancient term *Kyriake* (Day of the Lord). Another name for Sunday in the Greek liturgy is "Resurrection" (*Anastasis* in Greek, *Voskresenije* in Russian and Ukrainian). The Arabic-speaking Christians call it *Yom el-ahad* (the first day). The Maltese word *Il-Hadd* has the same meaning. The Lithuanians, on the other hand, call Sunday *Sekmádienis*, which means "the seventh day."

At the end of the sixteenth century the Puritans (Presbyterians and other sects) originated the somewhat confusing practice of calling Sunday "Sabbath," and thus began a custom which is still prevalent in the literature and sermons of some Protestant denominations.

The Christian Sunday worship in the early centuries consisted of two parts. The pagan Pliny the Younger (113), Governor of Bithynia, wrote in one of his letters to Emperor Trajan about this regular service of the Christians:

. . . that they used to meet on a certain fixed day before dawn, and to recite in alternating verses a hymn to Christ as to a god.[7]

This was the night vigil preceding the Sunday Mass. It consisted of sermons, prayers, the singing of hymns and psalms, and readings from Holy Scripture. (We still preserve this custom in the Epistle and Gospel of every Mass.) Then followed, in the early morning, the main act of worship—the Holy Sacrifice (*oblatio*). At its conclusion the faithful were dismissed. From this act (*Ite, missa est:* Go, now is the dismissal) the whole sacrifice came to be called *Missa* (Mass).

Eusebius (341), Bishop of Nicomedia, gives clear testimony about the celebration of Mass and the reception of Holy Communion in those early Christian centuries:

We, the children of the New Covenant, celebrate our Pasch every Sunday, being always nourished by the Body of the Savior, and always partaking of the Blood of the Lamb.

Every week on the Lord's day we observe the feast of our Pasch celebrating the mysteries of the true Lamb by Whom we have been redeemed.[8]

On the weekly day of our Savior's resurrection, which is called "Day of the Lord" [*Dominica*], you may see with your own eyes how those who receive the sacred food and salutary Body adore the Giver and Donor of this life-bestowing nourishment.[9]

The attendance at the Eucharistic Sacrifice was regarded as customary duty for all adult Christians in the third century.[10] Following the ancient custom of Jews and pagan Romans, the Christians put on their best clothes for attendance at worship. This tradition became universal among all Christian nations and has survived to our day even among those who no longer attend Sunday services.

Concerning Sunday rest, the Church naturally avoided what Christ had condemned as a narrow and

29

unreasonable interpretation of the law. But from the very beginnings the law itself was observed through the common conviction of Christians that all work must be discontinued that would make attendance at divine worship impossible or impede one's spiritual recollection on Sunday. The Council of Laodicaea stressed the obligation of Sunday rest for all Christians as far as possible though according to local tradition,[11] since different practices then prevailed in different places.

The duty of relieving slaves and servants from work so they could attend worship and instruction, both in the morning and in the afternoon, was universal. As early as the fourth century Christian masters even anticipated our modern week-end practice, for slaves were free from their duties even on Saturday, in preparation for Sunday.[12]

In early medieval times the obligation of resting from work began Saturday evening and used to be announced by the solemn ringing of church bells. Pope Alexander III (1181) declared that the time for Sunday rest could lawfully be reckoned from midnight to midnight, and today this practice is universally accepted.

The present demands of the Church regarding Sunday observance contain the grave obligation of attending Mass for all the faithful over seven years of age who are not excused by ill-health or other sufficient reasons.[13] The law of Sunday rest imposes the further obligation of abstaining from servile work (nonessential labor in household, farm, trade, industry), a custom that came directly from the practice regarding slaves, as the word "servile" denotes. Professional people, merchants, and civic officials are also required to abstain from their regular work. There are, though, many exceptions from the law because of present-day necessities, such as the duties of soldiers, policemen, firemen, doctors, nurses, officials, and workers in public utilities, communication, transportation, and similar occupations.[14]

The law does not apply to the so-called "liberal works" like study and writing, arts, music, sports, recreational activities, entertainment, nonlaborious hobbies, and similar pursuits. Apart from these technical details of ecclesiastical law, the Church has always stressed the positive ideal of Sunday observance. The Day of the Lord, after the public worship, should be spent in works of piety and charity, in peaceful relaxation, in the happy union of family life.

The first Christian emperor, Constantine, initiated the practice, which has continued through all the centuries up to our time, of honoring Sunday as the Day of the Lord by state laws and regulations. In 321 he forbade the sitting of courts and any legal action on Sunday. He also allowed all Christian soldiers to be excused from duty in order to attend Sunday service, while the pagan soldiers had to assemble in camp (without arms) and offer a prayer which he himself had composed.[15]

The emperors Theodosius (in 386) and Valentinian II (in 425) suppressed circus games and all theatrical shows on Sundays. In 400, Honorius (for West Rome) and Arcadius (for East Rome) forbade horse races on Sunday because they kept people from attending divine service. Emperor Leo I (474) of East Rome went so far as to forbid musical performances, both private and public. This prohibition, though, was soon again dropped from the lawbooks.

In later times the rulers of all European nations continued the Roman practice of regulating Sunday observance. In 596, the Merovingian King Childebert of the Franks issued a strict code of Sunday laws for the population of his realm. So did King Ine of Wessex (726) and King Wihtred of Kent (725) in England. In Germany the prescriptions of Sunday rest were incorporated in the Frankish, Bajuvarian, and Salian collections of law, in the eighth and ninth centuries.

Prior to the Reformation, sports and popular amusements were allowed on Sundays in England and Germany. Similarly, the duty of attendance at Sunday services was not under the sanction of the civil law but its enforcement was left to the spiritual authority of the Church. After the Reformation, however, when the power over the Church was vested in parliament and rulers, attendance at Sunday worship came to be enforced by the state. In England, the first act of this kind was passed under Edward VI, in 1551. Under Queen Elizabeth (1603) every adult citizen had to go to church on Sunday by order of the state or be fined a penalty of twelvepence. This law was not officially repealed until 1846.

The obligation of Sunday rest is still upheld by state law in all Christian countries. The legal tradition of England, which was also the basis for early American legislation, still tends toward greater severity than the observance of other nations. Gradually, though, most of the narrow civic restrictions ("blue laws") of past centuries are being removed from the lawbooks, and the present practice is more in keeping with modern conditions.

In the liturgical calendar of the Western Church, Sundays occupy a privileged position. Each Sunday has its own Mass text. There are, however, a few Sundays besides Easter and Pentecost which have a special feast assigned: the Sunday between New Year's and Epiphany (Feast of the Holy Name of Jesus), the Sunday after Epiphany (Feast of the Holy Family), the Sunday after Pentecost (Feast of the Holy Trinity), and the last Sunday in October (Feast of Christ the King).

In various countries certain feasts falling on a weekday are celebrated again with public solemnity on the following Sunday, like Corpus Christi (second Sunday after Pentecost), the Feast of the Sacred Heart of Jesus (third Sunday after Pentecost), the Feast of the Rosary (first Sunday in October), and the feasts of local or national patron saints.

The Greek Church celebrates a number of Sunday festivals, most of which are unfamiliar to Christians of the West, like the Feast of the Second Coming of the Lord, the Feast of the Holy Fathers of the Ecumenic Councils, the Feast of the Holy Patriarchs, and the Feast of All the Ancestors of Christ.[16]

In the folklore and tradition of most Christian nations Sunday is a day of good luck and special blessing. From early centuries the faithful considered it particularly consecrated to the Holy Trinity, and in many places they still light a lamp or candle in their homes before the picture of the Trinity every Sunday. Children born on Sunday are said to be gifted with a cheerful and happy disposition and followed by good fortune throughout their lives. Superstitions ascribe all kinds of unusual powers to them, such as seeing angels and other spirits, great power of persuasion, finding hidden treasures, and freedom from accidents.

On the other hand, people who violated the sanctity of Sunday were considered deserving of special punishments. Many legends of medieval times record such unusual happenings—Sunday violators being turned into stone, being frightened by a vision of the Devil, or being condemned to continue doing forever in the beyond what they had done while breaking the Sunday rest.

A touching custom still practiced in many Catholic sections of Europe is the "praying around the church" on Sunday after the Mass. People go through the churchyard sprinkling the graves with holy water and saying prayers for the souls of the departed.

In the early Middle Ages the common people, and many theologians, held the opinion that the suffering souls in purgatory, and even those in hell, enjoyed a considerable relief from their painful punishment of the senses every week from Saturday night until Monday morning, in honor of the Lord's Day. It was not until Saint Thomas Aquinas (1274) treated the problem in his masterful way, and disproved such opinions, that this claim was finally abandoned.[17]

Another interesting Sunday custom prevalent in many countries was, and still is, the "hearing" (*Abhören*) of the children at breakfast or dinner. During the meal the father gravely listens while the children repeat, as best they can, what the priest has preached in the Sunday sermon and what he has announced. If any corrections or explanations are in order, the mother usually provides them. Thus the parents make sure that the children have paid attention to the word of God and understand what was preached.

CHAPTER 2

The Feast of Pentecost

"And when the days of Pentecost were drawing to a close, they were all together in one place. And suddenly there came a sound from heaven, as of a violent wind coming, and it filled the whole house where they were sitting. And there appeared to them parted tongues as of fire, which settled upon each of them. And they were all filled with the Holy Spirit and began to speak in foreign tongues, even as the Holy Spirit prompted them to speak" (Acts 2, 1-4).

Whitsunday (Pentecost), with Christmas and Easter, ranks among the great feasts of Christianity. It commemorates not only the descent of the Holy Spirit upon the Apostles and Disciples but also the fruits and effects of that event: the completion of the work of redemption, the fullness of grace for the Church and her children, and the gift of faith for all nations.

The official name of the feast is "Pentecost." This word was already used in the Old Testament. It comes from the Greek *pentekoste* (the fiftieth), meaning the fiftieth day after Easter. On this day the Jews celebrated a great religious festival of thanksgiving for the year's harvest, the Feast of Firstfruits (see Ex. 23, 16). It was also called the Feast of Weeks because the day was reckoned by counting seven weeks after the Pasch (Lev. 23, 15-21). Being the second in importance of the festivals of the Old Testament, it annually drew large crowds of Jewish pilgrims from the Diaspora (dispersion) into Jerusalem. This fact is mentioned in the report of Saint Luke: "There were staying at Jerusalem devout Jews from every nation under heaven. . . ." (Acts 2, 5-11).

The Jews used the word Pentecost to indicate not only the feast itself but also the whole season of fifty days preceding it. In this sense Saint Luke mentions it in his Acts (2, 1): "When the days of Pentecost were drawing to a close. . . ." The early Christian Church accepted the Jewish usage and called the whole season from Easter to Whitsunday "Pentecost." It was a festive time of religious joy, no fasts were kept, and the faithful prayed standing in honor of Christ's Resurrection.

The feast itself was held annually from very early times. The famous writer Tertullian (third century) mentions it as a well-established Christian feast and as the second date for the solemn baptism of catechumens (the first being Easter).[18] Bishop Eusebius of Caesaria (339) calls it "all-blessed and all-holy [*panseptos kai panhagia*], the feast of feasts."[19] Saint John Chrysostom (407) uses similar phrases in his sermons on Pentecost: "Today we have arrived at the peak of all blessings, we have reached the capital [*metropolis*] of feasts, we have obtained the very fruit of our Lord's promise."[20]

During the early centuries just the day itself was celebrated in the Western Church. After the seventh century, however, the whole week came to be considered a time of festive observance. Law courts did not sit, and servile work was forbidden during the entire octave.[21] The Council of Constance (1094) limited this prohibition to three days. Pope Clement XIV, in 1771, abolished Tuesday as a prescribed holyday. Finally, in 1911, Pope Saint Pius X abolished Monday as a holyday of obligation; but most European countries, both Catholic and Protestant, still observe it as a legal holiday.

In most European languages the name of the feast comes from the ecclesiastical term: *Pentecôte* in French, *Pentecostés* in Spanish, *Pfingsten* in German, *Binkosti* in Slovenian, *Pünkösd* in Hungarian, *Pintse* in Danish, *Pentikosti* among the Slavs of the Eastern Church, and *Pentiqosti* in Syrian. A word meaning "Feast of the Holy Ghost" (*Duhovi, Turice*) is used by some Slavic nations including the Serbs, Croats, and Slovaks, and by the Rumanians (*Domineca Spiritului Santu*). The English word "Whitsunday" (White Sunday) originated because of the fact that the newly baptized appeared in white garments for the services of the day. Among the Arab-speaking Christians of the Near East the festival is called *'id el-'uncure* (Feast of the Solemn Assembly), the word coming from the Hebrew *'asereth* (festive meeting).[22]

Some nations have appropriately named the feast after the ancient custom of decorating homes and churches with flowers and boughs. This practice goes back to the nature lore of the Indo-European races. At the time of full spring, when trees stood in their early foliage and flowers blossomed in abundance, our pre-Christian ancestors celebrated a gay festival, with maypole, May Queen, and May dance, during which they adorned their homes with flowers and branches of pale-green tender leaves. This custom was retained in Christian times, and some of its features were transferred to the Feast of Pentecost. Thus the festival is called the "Green Holyday" (*Zielone Swieta*) in Poland and among the Ukrainians, "Flower Feast" (*Blumenfest*) in Germany, "Summer Feast" (*Slavnost Letnice*) among the Czechs. In the Latin countries a similar term is used: *Pascha Rosatum,* in Latin, meaning "Feast of Roses." The Italian name *Pascua Rossa* (Red Pasch) was inspired by the color of the liturgical vestments.

39

As early as the third century the vigil service of Whitsunday included the solemn rite of baptism in the Latin Church. On Saturday afternoon the catechumens gathered in church for prayers and preparation. The baptismal water was blessed by the bishop. All these ceremonies followed quite closely the ritual of the Easter vigil.[23] In some churches they even blessed a large candle and sang a hymn of praise (*praeconium*) as was done during the Easter vigil. These rites are no longer performed today.

There are no special liturgical ceremonies on Whitsunday apart from the Holy Sacrifice, which is usually celebrated with festive splendor and solemnity. In the Latin Church the color of the liturgical vestments is red, symbolizing the love of the Holy Spirit Who descended upon the Apostles in tongues of fire.

After the Gradual of the Mass the ancient sequence *Veni Sancte Spiritus* (Come, Holy Spirit) is recited or sung on each day of Pentecost week. This hymn appeared first in liturgical books around the year 1200. It has been variously ascribed to Pope Innocent III (1216), to King Robert of France (1031), and even to Saint Gregory the Great (604). Most probably, however, its author was Cardinal Stephen Langton (1128), Archbishop of Canterbury. The poem has been known from medieval times as the "Golden Sequence" because of its richness in thought and expression. Each one of the short stanzas is a sentence in itself, thus facilitating meditation.

Come, holy Ghost, and bring from above
  The splendor of thy light.

Come, father of the poor, come, giver of graces,
  Come, light of our hearts.

Best of consolers, sweet guest of the soul,
  And comfort of the weary.

Thou rest in labor, relief in burning toil,
  Consoling us in sorrow.

O blessed light, fill the innermost hearts
  Of those who trust in thee.

Without thy indwelling there is nothing in man,[24]
  And nothing free of sin.

Cleanse what is sordid, give water in dryness,
  And heal the bleeding wounds.

Bend what is proud, make warm what is cold,
  Bring back the wayward soul.

Give to the faithful who trustingly beg thee
  Thy seven holy gifts.

Grant virtue's reward, salvation in death,
  And everlasting joy. Amen. Alleluia.

Another liturgical hymn, which is used in the Divine Office, is the prayer-poem *Veni Creator Spiritus* (Come, Creator Spirit). It was probably written by Rabanus Maurus (856), Archbishop of Mainz, and has been widely used from the end of the tenth century on. Perhaps the best known among more than sixty English versions is the translation which John Dryden (1700) published in his book *Examen Poeticum* (1693):

> Creator Spirit, by whose aid
> The world's foundations first were laid,
> Come, visit every pious mind.
> Come, pour thy joy on human kind;
> From sin and sorrow set us free
> And make thy temples worthy Thee.

In addition to its place in the Pentecost liturgy, the *Veni Creator* has also been assigned as the official opening prayer for Church councils and synods. It is recited and sung by the faithful all over the world at the start of important undertakings, such as the beginning of a school year, at conventions, missions, retreats, and on many similar occasions. It is interesting to note that the *Veni Creator* is the only ancient Breviary hymn that has been retained in the official Prayer Book of the Protestant Episcopal Church (in the service of ordination).

In the churches of the Greek Rite a moving Vesper service is held on the evening of Whitsunday. After the joyful and festive note of the day, this evening service suddenly assumes the character of a sorrowful, penitential ceremony. In simple vestments of dark color the priests recite prayers of contrition and penance accompanied by humble prostrations and genuflections (*gonuklisia*). The purpose of this ancient ritual is to atone, at the end of the festive season, for all negligences and excesses that might have been committed during the fifty joyful days between Easter and Pentecost.[25]

From the earliest centuries of the Christian era preachers and writers have mentioned the dove as a symbol of the Holy Spirit. This symbolism, of course, was inspired by the Gospel report of Christ's baptism (Luke 3, 21-22). The Council of Constantinople (536) acknowledged the symbol for liturgical usage. As such it may be seen in churches, on priestly vestments, on altars, tabernacles, sacred utensils, and in many religious paintings.

In medieval times the figure of a dove was widely used to enact in a dramatic way the descent of the Holy Spirit on Pentecost Sunday. When the priest had arrived at the sequence, he sang the first words in a loud and solemn voice: *Veni Sancte Spiritus* (Come, Holy Ghost). Immediately there arose in the church a sound "as of a violent wind blowing" (Acts 2, 2). This noise was produced in some countries, like France, by the blowing of trumpets; in others by the choir boys, who hissed, hummed, pressed windbags, and rattled the benches. All eyes turned toward the ceiling of the church where from an opening called the "Holy Ghost Hole" there appeared a disc the size of a cart wheel, which slowly descended in horizontal position, swinging in ever-widening circles. Upon a blue background, broken by bundles of golden rays, it bore on its underside the figure of a white dove.

Meanwhile the choir sang the sequence. At its conclusion the dove came to rest, hanging suspended in the middle of the church. There followed a "rain" of flowers indicating the gifts of the Holy Spirit, and of water symbolizing baptism. In some towns of central Europe people even went so far as to drop pieces of burning wick or straw from the Holy Ghost Hole, to represent the flaming tongues of Pentecost. This practice, however, was eventually stopped because it tended to put the people on fire externally, instead of internally as the Holy Spirit had done at Jerusalem. In the thirteenth century in many cathedrals of France real white pigeons were released during the singing of the sequence and flew around in the church while roses were dropped from the Holy Ghost Hole.

Like all such religious pageants this dramatic addition to the liturgy of Whitsunday was attacked and ridiculed by the Lutheran reformers. Among other instances there is a report from the town of Biberach in Germany describing how in 1545 children broke the Holy Ghost Dove of the local church and carried the pieces in a mock procession through the streets.[26]

A fairly general custom in medieval times, and one still practiced in many sections of central and eastern Europe, is the use of artfully carved and painted wooden doves, representing the Holy Spirit. Usually this figure is suspended over the dining tables of rich and poor alike. Often it is encased in a globe of glass, into which it has been assembled with painstaking effort, a constant reminder for the members of the family to venerate the Holy Spirit.

Like Easter night, the night of Pentecost is considered one of the great "blessed nights" of the year. In many sections of Europe it is still the custom to ascend hill tops and mountains during the early dawn of Whitsunday to pray. People call this observance "catching the Holy Ghost." Thus they express in symbolic language the spiritual fact that only by means of prayer can the divine Dove be "caught" and the graces of the Holy Spirit obtained.

In rural sections of northern Europe superstitions ascribe a special power of healing to the dew that falls during Pentecost night. To obtain these blessings people walk barefoot through the grass on the early morning of the feast. They also collect the dew on pieces of bread which afterward are fed to their domestic animals as a protection against disease and accidents. In many places, all through Whitsunday night can be heard the noise of shooting (*Pfingstschiessen*) and cracking of whips (*Pfingstschnalzen*). In pre-Christian times this observance was held to frighten harmful powers away from home and harvest; in Christian times it assumed the character of a salute to the great feast.

The modern version of the ancient spring festival (maypole and May Queen) is connected with Pentecost in many sections of Europe. The queen is called

45

"Pentecost Bride" (*Pfingstbraut*). Other relics of the Indo-European spring festival are the games, dances, and races, held at Whitsuntide. This tradition used to be most popular everywhere in the Middle Ages, and still is in central Europe. In England, Pentecost Sunday was a day of horse races, plays, and feasting (Whitsun ale). In Germany, too, people would hold banquets (*Pfingstgelage*) and drink "Pentecost beer." Finally, there exists a Christian version of ancient nature lore in the custom of blessing flowers, fields, and fruit trees on the vigil of Pentecost.[27] In German-speaking countries the red peony (*paeonia officinalis*) bears the name *Pfingstrose* (Rose of Pentecost), and the oriole (*oriolus oriolus*) is called *Pfingstvogel* (Pentecost bird).

LITURGICAL PRAYER: *O God, who on this day didst instruct the hearts of Thy faithful through the light of the Holy Spirit: grant us in the same Spirit to understand what is right, and always to rejoice in His consolation.*[28]

CHAPTER 3

Trinity Sunday

The greatest dogma of the Christian faith is the mystery of the Holy Trinity. (Mystery, in this connection, means a supernatural fact revealed by God which in itself transcends the natural power of human reasoning.) During the first thousand years of Christianity there was no special feast celebrated in honor of this mystery but, as Pope Alexander II (1073) declared, every day of the liturgical year was devoted to the honor and adoration of the Sacred Trinity.[29]

The making of the sign of the Cross, which professes both faith in the Redemption of Christ and the Trinity, was practiced from the earliest centuries. Saint Augustine (431) mentions and describes it many times in his sermons and letters. In those days Christians made

47

the sign of the Cross (Redemption) with three fingers (Trinity) on their foreheads. The words ("In the name of the Father and the Son and the Holy Ghost") were added later. Almost two hundred years before Augustine, in the third century, Tertullian had already reported this touching and beautiful early Christian practice:

In all our undertakings—when we enter a place or leave it; before we dress; before we bathe; when we take our meals; when we light the lamps in the evening; before we retire at night; when we sit down to read; before each new task—*we trace the sign of the cross on our foreheads.*[30]

The ancient Christian doxology (prayer of praise) "Glory be to the Father, and to the Son, and to the Holy Ghost" was used in the Oriental Church. The second part ("as it was in the beginning . . .") seems to have been added at the time of Emperor Constantine. During the fifth century this beautiful short prayer came into the Western Church and spread very quickly. Since then it has been in constant use both in liturgical and private devotions. Finally, the Council of Narbonne (589) prescribed that it should be added after every psalm and hymn in the Divine Office. It is an ancient tradition that in poetical hymns of the liturgy the *Gloria Patri* is rendered in a paraphrase (free version) within the last stanza.

To counteract the Arian heresy, which denied the fullness of divinity to the Son, a special Mass text in

48

honor of the Holy Trinity was introduced and incorporated in the Roman liturgical books.[31] This Mass, however, was not assigned for a definite day but could be used on certain Sundays according to the private devotion of each priest. (Such Mass texts which are not prescribed but open to choice on certain days are now known as "Votive Masses.") From the ninth century on, various bishops of the Frankish kingdoms promoted in their own dioceses a special feast of the Holy Trinity, usually on the Sunday after Pentecost. They used a Mass text which Abbot Alcuin (804) had composed.

Thus the custom of observing a special feast in honor of the Trinity became increasingly popular in the northern countries of Europe. Several synods prescribed it for their respective territories in France, Germany, England, and The Netherlands. In the thirteenth century the orders of the Benedictines and Cistercians adopted the annual celebration of the feast. It was kept on different Sundays in different places, until in 1334 Pope John XXII accepted the festival into the official calendar of the Western Church and ordered that henceforth it should be held everywhere on the Sunday after Pentecost.

A new Mass text was written and published. It is interesting to note that the beautiful preface of the Trinity as read today is the same one that appeared in the first text of the Sacramentary of Saint Gregory the Great. Most of the other prayers are of later origin. The Divine Office, in its present form, was arranged under Pope Saint Pius V (1572). It is one of the most sublime offices of the Breviary.

The Feast of the Holy Trinity now belongs among the greatest annual festivals of Christianity. Although it is not observed with additional liturgical services outside the Mass, its celebration quickly took roots in the hearts and minds of the faithful, and in all countries of Europe popular traditions are closely associated with this feast.

During the first centuries of the Christian era the Holy Trinity was sometimes represented in paintings by three young men of identical shape and looks. However, the Council of Constantinople in 536 decreed that only the Father and Son should be shown in human form; the Holy Spirit was to be represented by the figure of a dove.

In medieval times there were many imaginative and symbolic pictures as well as designs to indicate the great mystery of the faith. The Church has not officially accepted any of them, has tolerated some, forbidden others. One of the best-known symbols of this kind is the trefoil (shamrock). A second plant to which this symbolism is attached is the pansy (*viola tricolor*), which even today is called "Trinity flower" in many parts of Europe. In Puerto Rico a delicately perfumed white flower with three petals is called "*Trinitaria*." Another symbol is the figure of a triangle (Trinity) surrounded by rays (Divinity) with the picture of an eye inside the triangle (Omniscience and Providence).

This design became very popular and may be found all over Europe in homes and on wayside shrines, even in churches. An interesting version of this symbol may be seen in the Great Seal of the United States (reproduced on every one-dollar bill).

Centuries ago, architecture made use of many, and sometimes strange, symbols to indicate the Trinity, like three animals (hares, stags, birds) in a circle, or three interlocked rings, or a candle with three flames. Some churches display an architectural number-symbolism in honor of the Trinity. One of the most remarkable examples of this kind is the Holy Trinity Church of Stadl-Paura, Austria, built in 1722. It has three aisles, three towers, three doors, three windows on either side, three altars, three bells, and three rows of pews.[32]

From the fourteenth century on the Holy Trinity was generally invoked for help against the dreaded epidemics of the Black Death. Hundreds of Trinity churches in Europe owe their existence to public vows made in time of pestilence and cholera. In subsequent ravages of those terrible diseases these churches became much-frequented pilgrim shrines. Later, during the seventeenth and eighteenth centuries, public columns in honor of the Holy Trinity were placed in the main squares of cities and towns in central Europe. Sculptured in marble or granite, they carry the traditional image of the Trinity, and statues of the saints who were patrons against epidemics. Many of these

51

columns are outstanding examples of late baroque art. The city of Vienna alone has eleven such Trinity columns which were erected during the epidemics of 1679 and 1713.

Whatever the weather on Trinity Sunday, it is said to be good and wholesome. "Trinity rain" is credited with special powers of health and fertility. Ghosts and witches are prevented from doing harm. Magic flowers blossom at midnight, bestowing on their finders all kinds of miraculous benefits like the healing of diseases, discovery of hidden treasures, protection against accidents, and freedom from pain for the rest of the year.

On the other hand, in popular phantasy the neglect or desecration of this great Sunday is punished with dire misfortune. Those who refuse to attend service or who do menial work will suffer sickness, accidents, or even death within the year. Any work with metal instruments (including sewing needles) will bring the additional punishment of drawing lightning upon the house for the rest of the season.

The churches of the Greek Rite do not celebrate the Feast of the Holy Trinity. Instead, they observe the Sunday after Pentecost as the Feast of All Saints (*Kyriake Ton Hagion Panton*). The official calendar of the Greek Church announces this feast with the interesting words: "Today, on the first Sunday after Pentecost, we celebrate the festive day of all Saints everywhere in the world: in Asia, Lybia, in Northern and

Eastern Europe." [33] As may be seen from the territories mentioned, the term "whole world" applies only to the countries of the Greek Rite.

LITURGICAL PRAYER: *Almighty, eternal God, who hast granted to Thy servants to acknowledge the glory of the eternal Trinity in the confession of true faith, and to worship the Unity in the power of Thy majesty: we beseech Thee, let us in the firmness of this faith be always protected against all adversities.*

CHAPTER 4

Corpus Christi

On Maundy Thursday, the day on which the Church
commemorates the institution of the Holy Eucharist,
it is impossible to honor the Blessed Sacrament with
appropriate solemn and joyful rites. Such a festival is
precluded by the sad and sorrowful memories of the
day—the betrayal of Judas, Christ's agony and ar-
rest, Peter's denial—and by the fact that other prescribed ceremonies are already occupying the time of
clergy and faithful on Holy Thursday.

It was a humble nun in Belgium, Saint Juliana
(1258), Prioress of Mont Cornillon, who first suggested
and advocated a special feast in honor of the Blessed
Sacrament to be celebrated on a day other than
Maundy Thursday. From her sixteenth year she had

54

often in her prayers beheld a strange sight: it was as if the full moon appeared to her in brilliant light, while a part of its disc remained black and lightless. Finally, in a vision, Christ showed her the meaning of this picture. The moon represented the ecclesiastical year; the black spot indicated the lack of a festival in honor of the Blessed Sacrament. She was to announce to the authorities of the Church that God wished such a feast to be established.

In 1230 Juliana communicated her secret to a small group of learned theologians. As her message became publicly known, she had to suffer scorn and ridicule for some years. But the bishop of her diocese (Liége) and some of his canons eventually lent a willing ear to her appeals. A diocesan synod in 1246 decided in her favor and prescribed such a feast for the churches of Liége.

Was it mere coincidence that one of the men who had supported her efforts in Belgium later became pope? He was Jacques Pantaléon, Archdeacon of Liége. Upon his election to the papal office he assumed the name of Urban IV (1261-1265). On September 8, 1264, six years after Juliana's death, he established for the whole Church that festival in honor of the Holy Eucharist which the saintly nun had proclaimed to be willed by God. It was to be celebrated with great solemnity on the Thursday after Pentecost week, and indulgences were granted to all who would receive Holy

Communion or attend special devotions in addition to hearing Mass.[34]

Urban IV commissioned the great Dominican scholar Saint Thomas Aquinas to compose the texts of Mass and Divine Office for the new feast. The splendor, depth, and devotion of the prayers and hymns which Saint Thomas wrote have enriched the liturgy with one of its most beautiful rituals. They are still in use today, admired and appreciated by people of all faiths.

The bull of Urban IV had no immediate effect because he died soon after its publication, and the succeeding popes did not urge the matter. Finally, however, Pope Clement V in 1314 renewed the decrees in a bull of his own, and then the feast spread quickly throughout the Latin Church.[35] Later it was also accepted by some parts of the Oriental Church (Syrians, Armenians, Copts, and Melchites). The churches of the Greeks, Ukrainians, and Russians (of the Greek Catholic Rite) do not celebrate this feast.

The official title of the feast is, in the Latin Church, *Festum Sanctissimi Corporis Christi* (Feast of the Most Holy Body of Christ). In the Greek Church it is called *Tou Somatos Tou Kyriou Heorte* (Feast of the Body of the Lord). From these ecclesiastical terms many Christian nations have adopted popular names for the feast, like the English and Spanish *Corpus Christi*, the German *Fronleichnam* (Body of the Lord), the Slavic *Boze Telo* (Body of God), the Syriac *pagre d' maran* (Body of the Lord), and the Arabic *'id el-jesed el-*

ilahi (Feast of the Body of God). Other names are, *Fête Dieu* (Feast of God) in French, *Úrnapja* (Day of the Lord) in Hungary, *Brasancevo* (Sacred Bread) among the southern Slavs.

Very early (in the fourteenth century) the custom developed of carrying the Blessed Sacrament in a splendid procession through the town after the Mass on Corpus Christi Day. This was encouraged by the popes, some of whom granted special indulgences to all participants.[36] The Council of Trent (1545-1563) solemnly approved and recommended the procession on Corpus Christi as a public profession of the Catholic faith in the real presence of Christ in the Holy Sacrament.[37]

During the later Middle Ages these processions developed into splendid pageants of devotion and honor to the Blessed Sacrament. They are still publicly held, and often with the ancient splendor, in Italy, France, Spain, Portugal, Austria, Belgium, Ireland, in the Catholic sections of Germany, Holland, Switzerland, Canada, Hungary, and in the Slavic countries and South America. Sovereigns and princes, presidents and ministers of the state, magistrates, members of trade and craft guilds, honor guards of the armed forces, accompany the liturgical procession while the church bells peal, bands play sacred hymns, and the faithful kneel in front of their homes to adore the Eucharistic Lord. The houses along the route of the procession are decorated with little birch trees and green boughs. Candles and pictures adorn the windows; and in many places, especially in Latin countries, the streets are covered with carpets of grass and flowers, often wrought in beautiful designs.[38]

A special and appealing ritual in the procession is an adaptation of the ancient Roman usage of "stations." Stops are made at various points along the route, the Blessed Sacrament is put on an altar table, and a passage of the Gospel is sung, followed by a hymn and a liturgical prayer for God's blessing upon the town, the people, and the harvest. A Eucharistic benediction concludes each "station." This ritual, approved by Pope Martin V (1431), is still observed everywhere in the Catholic sections of central Europe and in some Latin countries.[39]

In most European countries mystery plays used to be performed after the procession in public squares or in churches. These Corpus Christi pageants were highly popular, especially in England, Germany, and Spain. Perhaps the most famous of them are the *Autos Sacramentales* (Plays of the Sacrament) by the Spanish priest and poet Pedro Calderón de la Barca (1681). They are still performed today on special occasions such as centenary celebrations, Eucharistic congresses, and ecclesiastical jubilees.

The solemnity of the Corpus Christi festival is enhanced by the additional use of "alleluia" in the prayers of the liturgy (as at Easter time). Saint Thomas Aquinas has magnificently expressed the jubilant char-

58

acter of the day in his famous hymns, especially in *Sacris Solemniis*, which is recited during the matins of the feast and sung at the procession:

> *Sacris solemniis juncta sint gaudia,*
> *Et ex praecordiis sonent praeconia;*
> *Recedant vetera, nova sint omnia,*
> *Corda, voces et opera.*

Great is the festive day, joyful and jubilant,
Let us with loving hearts offer the song of praise;
Freed from the sinful past, may we renew in grace
All our thoughts and words and deeds.

The fifth stanza of *Sacris Solemniis* has been used for centuries as a separate hymn in honor of the Blessed Sacrament. As *Panis Angelicus* (Bread of the Angels) it is known and cherished widely among Christians of many denominations. The best musical settings are those of César Franck (1890), of the French Jesuit Louis Lambilotte (1855), and the powerful four-part setting usually ascribed to C. Casiolini which, however, should be more correctly credited to Jacopo Tomadini (1883).

Another hymn by Saint Thomas, *Pangue Lingua Gloriosi Corporis Mysterium* (Praise, o tongue, the mystery of the glorious Body) contains the two stanzas which are sung all over the world at every Eucharistic service, *Tantum Ergo* and *Genitori*. The best known, and perhaps most beautiful, of any musical settings has remained the Gregorian Chant tune (Mode III):

59

Tantum ergo sacramentum
Veneremur cernui,
Et antiquum documentum
Novo cedat ritui.
Praestet fides supplementum
Sensuum defectui.

Genitori genitoque
Laus et jubilatio,
Salus, honor, virtus quoque
Sit, et benedictio.
Procedenti ab utroque
Compar sit laudatio. Amen.

For the Lauds of Corpus Christi, Aquinas wrote the hymn *Verbum Supernum Prodiens* (The Divine Word coming forth). Again the last stanza preceding the customary conclusion in praise of the Trinity has become a favorite song and prayer in itself:

> *O salutaris hostia,*
> *Quae caeli pandis ostium,*
> *Bella praemunt hostilia:*
> *Da robur, fer auxilium.*

> O saving host, o bread of life,
> Thou goal of rest from pain and strife,
> Embattled are we, poor and weak:
> Grant us the strength and help we seek.

Finally, there is the sequence of the Mass, *Lauda Sion Salvatorem* (Sion, praise thy Lord and Saviour). Saint Thomas enumerates in unmistakable words the main truths of Christ's revelation and the Church's teaching about the Holy Eucharist. In many countries a translation of this sequence into the vernacular is sung by the people as a popular church hymn in honor of the Blessed Sacrament.

The most famous nonliturgical hymn in honor of the Blessed Sacrament is the ancient prayer-poem *Ave Verum Corpus* (Hail, true Body). It appeared first in manuscripts at the end of the fourteenth century and is ascribed to Pope Innocent VI (1362). Its original purpose was to serve as a private prayer for the faithful to be said at the elevation of the sacred Host during Mass

(*In elevatione Corporis Christi*). This jewel of sacred poetry soon spread through most Catholic countries of Europe. It became famous also among other Christians through the musical setting of exquisite beauty written by Mozart (1791). Other familiar musical arrangements are those of Gounod (1893) and Saint-Saëns (1921).

The Polish people have an ancient hymn in honor of the Blessed Sacrament, *Twoja Czesc Chwala*, which they sing at Corpus Christi and on other occasions at Eucharistic devotions. Tune and text are traditional.

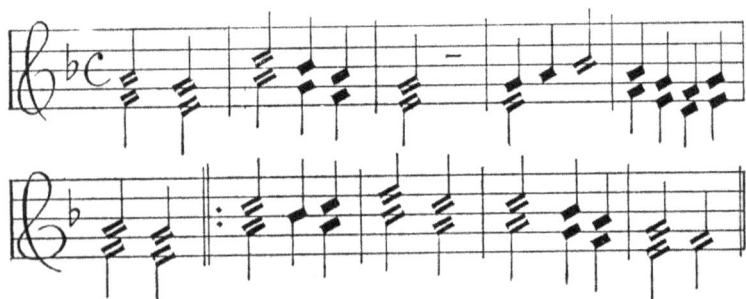

Thy praise and glory,
O Lord triumphant,
Through all the ages
Resound exultant.

In this our exile
Forever near us,
O Lord, from the altar
Do graciously hear us.

Receive our tribute
Of thanks and laudation,
O Sacrament holy,
O Bread of Salvation.

In central Europe, and also in France, Corpus Christi Day is the "Day of Wreaths" (*Kranzeltag*) and of huge bouquets of flowers borne on the top of wooden poles (*Prangtag*). Wreaths and bouquets of exquisite flowers in various colors are attached to flags and banners, to houses, and to the arches of green boughs that span the streets. The clergy and altar boys wear little wreaths on their left arms in the procession; girls carry wreaths on their heads. Even the monstrance containing the Blessed Sacrament is adorned with a wreath of choice flowers on Corpus Christi Day. In Poland these wreaths are blessed by the priest on the eve of the feast day. After the solemnities people decorate their homes with them. Some are suspended on the walls of the houses or affixed to doors and windows. Others are put up in gardens, fields, and pastures, with a prayer for protection and blessing upon the growing harvest.

In the New World the Feast of Corpus Christi was celebrated during the sixteenth and seventeenth centuries, with the usual solemn observance, by the missionaries and their native converts in Florida, California, Texas, New Mexico, and in the missions of New France (Canada and the Great Lakes region). In honor of the festival the Franciscans named a bay of the Mexican Gulf "Corpus Christi Bay." Later a town, founded on the shore of that bay, was given the same title—Corpus Christi, Texas. In a similar way the capital of California was named Sacramento after the river on which it is situated, which had been named by the missionaries in honor of the Holy Eucharist.

The discoverer of Lake George in upper New York State was the Jesuit missionary and martyr Saint Isaac Jogues (1646). The first white man to come upon the lake, he named it "Lake of the Blessed Sacrament" because he had said Mass on one of its islands during Corpus Christi season (May, 1646). The lake retained this name until, in 1755, over a hundred years later, a colonial governor, William Johnson, renamed it in honor of King George II of England.

LITURGICAL PRAYER: *O God, who hast left us in this admirable sacrament a memorial of Thy passion, grant us to venerate the holy mysteries of Thy Body and Blood in such a way that we may ever perceive in us the fruit of Thy redemption.*

CHAPTER 5

Thanksgiving

The religious function of giving thanks to Divinity for favors received is as old as humanity. In fact, it is one of the basic elements of worship in all religions, flowing directly from the moral Law of Nature which governs the relation of man to God and attaches a fourfold purpose to the acts of worship: adoration, petition, atonement, thanksgiving. Thus we find sacrifices and thanksgiving rites as far back as we have documentary and archaeological evidence on the purpose of any forms of worship.

The Jews in the Old Testament had an elaborate ritual of sacrifices and offerings in thanksgiving to God. The details of these thank-offerings are prescribed in the Law of Moses (Lev. 1, 2, 3, 7, etc.). They were either private acts of thanksgiving on the part of individuals or public acts of worship offered in the name of the whole community. The gifts offered consisted of the sacrificing of animals or the presentation of ritual loaves, cakes, and wafers.

In the New Testament, also, the Sacrifice of the Mass contains the same fourfold purpose prescribed by Natural Law. The function of thanksgiving has never been overlooked. The early Christians were so much aware of it that they called the Blessed Sacrament, which is offered in the Mass, *Eucharist* (thanksgiving). Due to the fact that the Holy Sacrifice is the greatest act of thanksgiving that could possibly be offered to God, the Church has refrained from instituting any special feast or liturgical ceremony of thanksgiving other than the Mass. In the Catholic Church, liturgically speaking, every day of the year is "Thanksgiving Day."

There is, however, the psychological need of special manifestations of thanksgiving for the people on certain occasions. In such cases, as at the end of an epidemic, or liberation from a threatened disaster, or conclusion of peace, great celebrations of thanksgiving have been held since medieval times. As far as their religious significance is concerned, they consist either in a Mass of thanksgiving celebrated with unusual splendor and solemnity or in a service of Benediction of the Blessed Sacrament. At the end of such services it is customary to recite or sing the ancient (fifth century) hymn, *Te Deum Laudamus* (God, we praise thee), and to add the liturgical Mass prayer of thanks-giving.

A free translation in the vernacular, "Holy God, we praise Thy name," is often sung on such occasions. The English text is a translation from the German. The author of this hymn was Johann Franz (1790), and the tune is taken from a cantata of K. Bone (1852):

> Holy God, we praise thy name,
> Lord of all, we bow before thee;
> All on earth thy sceptre claim,
> All in Heav'n above adore thee.
> Infinite thy vast domain,
> Everlasting is thy reign.
>
> Hark, the loud celestial hymn
> Angel choirs above are raising;
> Cherubim and Seraphim,
> In unceasing chorus praising,
> Fill the Heavens with sweet accord:
> Holy, holy, holy Lord.

One special, and yearly, thanksgiving celebration going back to ancient times took place at the successful conclusion of the harvest. That is why we find harvest festivals with thanksgiving rites everywhere as far back as we can go in our knowledge of religions and cultures. Among the Indo-European races it was the great "Mother of Grains" to whom these rites were addressed. Within the various ancient nations this common mythological Mother of Fields was represented as a national god or goddess of vegetation (Astarte, Osiris, Tammuz, Demeter, Ceres). Great festivals were held every year in their honor in thanksgiving for the harvest. The most famous of all these feasts were the Eleusinian Mysteries in Greece, held every September as a tribute to the grain goddess Demeter.

Among the Slavic, Germanic, and Celtic races the ancient belief in the great "Mother of Grains" has persisted to our day in the form of many superstitious practices connected with fall harvesting, especially with the "last sheaf" in every field. Sometimes the sheaf is personified, molded into the form of a straw doll and, as "harvest baby," carried in joyful procession from the field to the village. In Austria it is shaped into a wreath and placed on the head of a girl who then is designated at the harvest festival as "queen" or "bride" (*Erntebraut*). Similar customs were universally practiced in England, where the last load brought home with great rejoicing bore the name "horkey cart," and in Scotland, where the last sheaf is called "kirn [grain] doll."

In northern France harvesters, seated on top of the last load brought home from the fields, chant an ancient traditional tune to the text *"Kyre-o-ôle."* This is an interesting relic of folklore from Carolingian times when shepherds and field workers cheered their solitary toil by singing the *Kyrie Eleison* as they had heard the monks sing it at High Mass. In southern France the last sheaf was tied in the form of a cross, decorated with ribbons and flowers, and after the harvest celebration was placed in the best room of the house to be kept as a token of blessing and good fortune.

Moses had already instituted among the Jews two great religious feasts of thanksgiving for the harvest: the Feast of the Spring Harvest (*Hag Shavu'oth*, Feast of Weeks, or Pentecost; Lev. 23, 15-21) and the Feast of the Fall Harvest (*Sukkoth*, Feast of Tabernacles; Lev. 29-43):

Thou shalt celebrate the festival of weeks to the Lord thy God, a voluntary oblation of thy hand which thou shalt offer according to the blessing of the Lord thy God. And thou shalt feast before the Lord thy God, thou and thy son, and thy daughter, and thy manservant, and thy maidservant, and the Levite that is within thy gates, and the stranger and the fatherless, and the widow, who abide with you in the place . . . (Deut. 16, 9-11).

Thou also shalt celebrate the solemnity of tabernacles seven days, when thou hast gathered in thy fruit of the barnfloor and of the winepress. And thou shalt make merry in thy festival time, thou, thy son, and thy daughter, thy manservant, and thy maidservant, the Levite also and the stranger, and the fatherless and the widow that are within thy gates (Deut. 16, 13-15).

In the Christian era the custom of celebrating a thanksgiving harvest festival began in the High Middle Ages. For lack of any definite liturgical day or ceremony prescribed by the Church, various practices came

69

to be observed locally. In many places, as in Hungary, the Feast of the Assumption included great thanksgiving solemnities for the grain harvest. Delegates from all parts of the country came for the solemn procession to Budapest, carrying the best samples of their produce. A similar ceremony was observed in Poland, where harvest wreaths brought from all sections to Warsaw were bestowed on the president in a colorful pageant. These wreaths (*wieniec*), made up of the straw of the last sheaf (*broda*), were beautifully decorated with flowers, apples, nuts, and ribbons, and blessed in churches by the priests.

The most common, and almost universal, harvest and thanksgiving celebration in medieval times was held on the Feast of Saint Martin of Tours (Martinmas) on November 11. It was a holiday in Germany, France, Holland, England, and in central Europe. People first went to Mass and observed the rest of the day with games, dances, parades, and a festive dinner, the main feature of the meal being the traditional roast goose (Martin's goose). With the goose dinner they drank "Saint Martin's wine," which was the first lot of wine made from the grapes of the recent harvest. Martinmas was the festival commemorating filled barns and stocked larders, the actual Thanksgiving Day of the Middle Ages. Even today it is still kept in rural sections of Europe, and dinner on Martin's Day would be unthinkable without the golden-brown, luscious Martin's goose.

The tradition of eating goose as part of the Martin's Day celebration was kept in Holland even after the Reformation. It was there that the Pilgrims who sailed to the New World in 1620 became familiar with this ancient harvest festival. When, after one year in America, they decided to celebrate a three days' thanksgiving in the autumn of 1621, they went in search of geese for their feast. We know that they also had deer (a present from the Indians), lobsters, oysters, and fish. But Edward Winslow, in his account of the feast, only mentions that "Governor Bradford sent foure men on fowling that so we might after a more speciall manner rejoice together, after we had gathered the fruit of our labours." They actually did find some wild geese, but a number of wild turkeys and ducks as well.

The Pilgrim Fathers, therefore, in serving wild turkeys with the geese, inaugurated one of the most cherished American traditions: the turkey dinner on Thanksgiving Day. They also drank, according to the ancient European tradition, the first wine of their wild grape harvest. Pumpkin pie and cranberries were not part of the first Thanksgiving dinner in America but were introduced many years afterward.

The second Thanksgiving Day in the New World was held by the Pilgrims two years later, on July 30, 1623. It was formally proclaimed by the governor as a day of prayer to thank God for their deliverance from drought and starvation, and for the safe arrival from Holland of the ship *Anne*.

71

In 1665 Connecticut proclaimed a solemn day of thanksgiving to be kept annually on the last Wednesday in October. Other New England colonies held occasional and local Thanksgivings at various times. In 1789 the federal Congress authorized and requested President George Washington to proclaim a day of thanksgiving for the whole nation. Washington did this in a message setting aside November 26, 1789 as National Thanksgiving Day.

After 1789 the celebration reverted to local and regional observance for almost a hundred years. There grew, however, a strong desire among the majority of the people for a national Thanksgiving Day that would unite all Americans in a festival of gratitude and public acknowledgment for all the blessings God had conferred upon the nation. It was not until October 3, 1863, that President Lincoln issued, in the midst of the Civil War, a Thanksgiving Proclamation. In it the last Thursday of November was set apart for that purpose and made a national holiday.

Since then, every president has followed Lincoln's example, and annually proclaims as a "Day of Thanksgiving" the fourth Thursday in November. Only President Franklin D. Roosevelt changed the date, in 1939, from the fourth to the third Thursday of November (to extend the time of Christmas sales). This caused so much consternation and protest that in 1941 the traditional date was restored.

The original meaning and purpose of the ancient harvest feast has not only been preserved but broadened and elevated into a national tribute of deeply religious significance. This fact is impressed on anyone who reads George Washington's proclamation:

Whereas it is the duty of all nations to acknowledge the providence of Almighty God, to obey his will, to be grateful for his benefits, and humbly to implore his protection and favor . . .

Now therefore I do recommend and assign Thursday, the twenty-sixth of November next, to be devoted by the people of these States to the service of that great and glorious Being, who is the Beneficent Author of all good that was, that is, or that will be;

That we may then all unite in rendering unto him our sincere and humble thanks for his kind care and protection of the people of this country . . .

For the civil and religious liberty with which we are blessed, and the means we have of acquiring and diffusing useful knowledge; and, in general, for all the great and various favors, which he has been pleased to confer upon us.

And also, that we may then unite in most humbly offering our prayers and supplications to the great Lord and Ruler of Nations, and beseech him to pardon our national and other transgressions;

To enable us all, whether in public or private institutions, to perform our several and relative duties properly and punctually;

To render our National Government a blessing to all the people, by constantly being a government of wise, just, and constitutional laws, discreetly and faithfully executed and obeyed . . .

To promote the knowledge and practice of true religion and virtue, and the increase of science . . .

And, generally, to grant unto all mankind such a degree of temporal prosperity as he alone knows to be best.

LITURGICAL PRAYER: *O God, Thy mercies are without number, and the treasure of Thy goodness is infinite: we offer thanks to Thy most gracious majesty for the gifts Thou hast bestowed upon us, and we continue to implore Thy kindness that, having granted the petitions asked of Thee, Thou wilt never forsake those who pray but prepare them for the reward to come.*

Feasts of Saints

CHAPTER 6

The Veneration of Saints

The Bible, in the book of the Apocalypse, mentions various kinds of "saints": the virgins (14, 1-5), the prophets and Apostles (18, 20), the martyrs for the word of God (6, 9), the martyrs of Jesus (17, 6), and all those who died in the Lord and whose good works follow them (14, 13).

The custom of calling the death date of a martyr his "birthday" (*Dies Natalis*) originated in the early centuries. It expresses the truth that any Christian who remained loyal to the Lord unto the death of martyrdom is truly born into eternal glory at the hour of his execution. The official calendars both of the Eastern and Western Churches have retained this practice to our day. When they announce the "birthday" of a saint it means the day of his death. The only exceptions are the natural birthdays of the three persons who were born into this world without original sin: Christ, Mary, and John the Baptist. Of these three the Church celebrates their earthly nativity as well as the day of death.

During the persecutions in the Roman Empire each community commemorated only its local martyrs. Their names and the dates of their execution were carefully recorded, and each church kept the official list of its heroes. In larger places like Rome, Christian notaries were appointed for the various districts (*regiones*) of the city. It was their task to observe and record all cases of executions of Christians in their particular district. Thus came into existence the venerable catalogues of martyrs in the various cities of the Roman Empire. They were not only read at divine service, but were often engraved on tablets of marble and set up as a public notice for the faithful, to remind them to honor and venerate their local saints.

Concerning the graves of the early martyrs, there is no doubt that the great majority of them remained well identified. According to Roman law, up to the time of Diocletian (305), even executed criminals were entitled to an honorable burial, for earthly justice was satisfied by the death of the guilty person. The body usually was granted to relatives or friends to be duly buried.[40] Thus the tombs of the saints were naturally well known to the bishops and faithful, for in many cases they themselves had selected the burial place, given the last honors to the sacred bodies, and laid them to rest with their own hands. A tradition based on the certitude of such direct evidence is not easily lost even in the course of centuries. This was confirmed by the results of recent research and excavations in various places.

However, with the increasing number and scope of persecutions, many martyrs remained unlisted, neither could all anniversaries be kept even within a particular community. For this reason only the outstanding few received an established annual feast of memorial services. All the others shared one great feast in common, to give due honor and recognition to their memory every year. This was the "Feast of All Martyrs," instituted in the Eastern Church in the fifth century, and adopted by Rome in the seventh century. Its title was later changed to "Feast of All Saints."

In the third century the bishops began also listing the names of persons who did not reach the point of execution but died a natural death after having suffered persecution for the sake of Christ, like Saint Nicholas, who had been in prison for many years but was finally released in 312 at the end of the persecutions. These saints were added to the list under the name of "confessors," because they had heroically confessed their faith before the tribunals. This term has remained in official use up to the present. It now designates any male saint who through the practice of heroic virtue gave witness to Christ. Holy women are identified in liturgical usage as "martyrs" or "virgins" or "virgins and martyrs" or "neither virgins nor martyrs" (a somewhat unfortunate negative term meaning those who became saints as wives and mothers).

In medieval times a much greater number of saints' days were holydays of obligation than are now. First among them ranked the five major feasts of Mary, of which only two have remained prescribed holydays. The days of all the Apostles were raised to the rank of public holydays in 932. The feasts of Saint Michael, Saint Stephen, Saint John the Baptist, and other saints of the early centuries were celebrated in the past as holydays among all Christian nations.

Still another group of holydays is made up of the feasts of those saints who were (and are) special patron saints in certain localities. This group comprises hundreds of saints, often little known to the rest of the world. Every parish, diocese, ecclesiastical province, every religious institution and community has its particular heavenly patron. So have most nations, states, regions, cities, and towns. In each place the feast of the patron saint used to be kept as a true holyday. The present Canon Law provides for the continuation of this practice, though only from the liturgical aspect; the day of the patron saint may be celebrated as a religious solemnity but not as a holyday of obligation (unless prescribed for the whole Church).[41] In many countries people are still accustomed to the patron's feast as it used to be kept in past centuries. It is now usually held on the Sunday following the liturgical feast. They observe it with great devotion and rejoicing. The whole day, after the service, is spent in celebration consisting of processions, parades, and traditional pageants, fairs, amusements, banquets, and dancing. This festival is called *Kirmes* in German, *Bucsu* in Hungarian, *Kermes* in Slovak, *Pokrove* in Russian and Ukrainian, *Fête Patronale* in French, *Fiesta del Patrono* in Spanish.

A permanent civic testimony to the patronage of saints are the names of countless towns and cities in all Christian lands. In the United States over ninety cities, towns, and counties bear the names of saints. As might be expected, the most frequent title is that of the Blessed Virgin (St. Marys, Santa Maria, etc.); then follows the name John (St. Johns, San Juan, etc.) and Saint Clair (St. Clare, Santa Clara, etc.).

The most significant patronal feasts are, of course, the days of national patron saints which are celebrated by the faithful of an entire country or race. Liturgically speaking, they are in most cases "secondary" patrons because the Blessed Virgin is the primary patron in the majority of Christian countries. In Catholic nations, and in Catholic sections of Protestant countries, these days are still observed, in some cases even as legal holidays.

The best known of these national and regional patron saints are: Anthony of Padua (Portuguese and Italians), James the Great (Spaniards), Patrick (Irish),

81

George (Chaldeans, Greeks, Portuguese, English), Canute (Danes), Olaf (Swedes and Norwegians), Louis (French), Stephen the King (Hungarians), Michael (Germans, Basques), Cyril and Methodius (Slavs), Nicholas (Russians, Dutch), Boniface (Germans), Joseph (Austrians, Canadians), American Martyrs (United States), Rose of Lima (South Americans), Thomas the Apostle (Indians), Ephraem (Syrians), Gregory (Armenians), Josaphat (Ukrainians), Stanislaus (Poles), Elias (Yugoslavians), Francis Xavier (Japanese), Martyrs of Uganda (Africans).

There is a third group of saints' days that are observed as holydays, but only privately, within the family and among friends and neighbors. It was a general custom before the Reformation, and still is in Catholic countries, to celebrate not so much the birthday but rather the feast of the saint whose name was received in baptism. This "baptismal saint" is considered a special and personal patron all through life. Children are made familiar with the history and legend of "their own" saint, are inspired by his life and example, pray to him every day, and gratefully accept his loving help in all their needs. It is a beautiful custom, this close relationship of an individual to his personal patron saint in Heaven.

On the feast of such a saint, called "Name Day," all who bear that name usually attend Mass. Upon their return from the church the whole family congratulates them, offering not only good wishes but little presents as well. Then all sit down to a festive breakfast at the gaily decorated table. For the one whose feast day it is the rest of the day is free from regular chores and duties in household or farming and is spent in the manner and mood of a true holiday.

The favorite cake for the Name Day is baked in a fluted tube pan and is called *Napfkuchen* in Germany, *Guglhupf* in Austria, *Kuglof* in Hungary, and *Babka* among the Slavic nations. Here is its recipe:

½ cup heavy cream	4 egg yolks
1 cake of yeast	4 egg whites
7 oz. fine flour	3 oz. raisins
5 oz. butter	3 oz. almonds
2½ oz. sugar	salt
grated rind of 1 lemon	

Beat butter until creamy, add flour, salt, egg yolks, sugar, yeast, and, last, cream and chopped almonds. Beat half-hour, until batter drops from spoon. Add stiffly beaten egg whites. Mix well again. Put mixture into greased and preheated form (fluted pan). Put in warm place and let rise to about double size. Bake about one hour in moderate oven. Take out of form and sprinkle with sugar while still warm.

The custom of giving children the names of Christian saints dates from the first millennium. It was especially in the Frankish kingdoms (France and Germany) that people began a more general practice of assuming for themselves, or bestowing upon their children, the names of Apostles and other Biblical saints, of early martyrs and confessors. By the thirteenth century this custom was fairly widespread on the continent of Europe.

In Ireland, however, the Gaelic population did not follow this custom. It is interesting to note that no Christian names are found in the ancient Irish documents. No names of native saints, not even the name of their beloved patron, Saint Patrick, were given to their children in those early centuries. This fact is explained by the devout and humble attitude of the Gaelic people. They would have considered it an act of irreverence to claim such hallowed names for their own. This practice remained an established tradition until after the advent of the Normans. The Continental practice began to prevail by the thirteenth century.

Some Gaelic clans, however, called themselves the "servants" (*gil, mal*) of our Lord and the saints. Hence the modern surnames like Gilmartin (servant of Saint Martin), Malone (servant of Saint John), Gilpatrick (servant of Saint Patrick), Gilmary (servant of Mary), Gilchrist (servant of Christ), Gillis (servant of Jesus).[42]

Another interesting custom is that of the Spanish-speaking people naming boys "Jesus" after the sacred name of the Lord. All other Christian nations have refrained from doing so through a feeling of special reverence (just as the popes have always refrained from assuming the name of Peter). In similar fashion the Irish used to set apart and keep sacred the original name of Mary (Muire), never bestowing it on their daughters in this form. All girls who received the name of the Blessed Virgin bore it in other forms (mostly Maire).[43]

It is a general custom in Spanish-speaking countries to use not only the name of Mary but also some of her liturgical titles and attributes as girls' names, like Dolores (Our Lady of Sorrows), Luz (Our Lady of Light), Paz (Our Lady of Peace), Concepción or Chonca (Immaculate Conception), Asunción (Assumption), Pura (Virgin Most Pure), Victoria (Our Lady of Victory), Consuelo (Our Lady of Good Counsel), Gracia (Our Lady of Grace), Stella (Star of the Sea), and others. Some of these Spanish names, like Dolores, Grace, Stella, and Victoria, have been adopted into English and American usage.

A similar custom prevails among the Chaldeans and Syrians where, besides our Lady's name (Miriam), other names referring to Mary are given to girls in baptism: Kamala (Mary's perfection), Jamala (her beauty), 'Afifa (her purity), Farida (her uniqueness), and similar words expressing her attributes.

In our day when even Christian parents often choose their children's names without regard to hallowed traditions, the Church still strongly recommends the bestowing of a saint's name in baptism, at least as middle name whenever the chosen first name is not of Christian origin or significance.

CHAPTER 7

Candlemas

The Law of Moses prescribed that every Jewish mother after giving birth to a boy child was to be excluded from attendance at public worship for forty days. At the end of that period she had to present a yearling lamb for a holocaust and a pigeon for sin-offering, thus purifying herself from ritual uncleanliness. In the case of poor people, two pigeons sufficed as an offering (Lev. 12, 2-8). The Gospel reports how Mary, after the birth of Jesus, fulfilled this command of the Law, and how on the same occasion Simeon and Anna met the newborn Saviour (Luke 2, 22-38).

Since Christ Himself was present at this event, it came to be celebrated quite early as a festival of the Lord. The first historical description of the feast is given in the diary of Egeria, a lady from the Roman province of Spain, who made a pilgrimage to the Holy Land in 380. She mentions that the services in Jerusalem began with a solemn procession in the morning, followed by a sermon on the Gospel text of the day, and finally Mass was offered. At that time the festival was kept on February 14, because the birth of Christ was celebrated on the Feast of the Epiphany (January 6). It had no special name but was called "the fourtieth day after Epiphany." [44]

From Jerusalem the feast spread into the other churches of the Orient. The Armenians call it the "Coming of the Son of God into the Temple" and still celebrate it on February 14. In the Coptic (Egyptian) Rite it is termed "Presentation of the Lord in the Temple." East Roman Emperor Justinian I in 542 prescribed it for the whole country as a public holyday, in thanksgiving for the end of a great pestilence. By that time it was known in the Greek Church under the title *Hypapante Kyriou* (The Meeting of the Lord), in commemoration of Christ's meeting with Simeon and Anna.

According to the Gospel, Simeon, holding the Child in his arms, said, "Now doest thou dismiss thy servant, o Lord. . . ." The word "now" prompted the Christians of the Orient to believe that Simeon, having seen the Saviour, died on the same day. Thus they made Candlemas also the annual feast of Simeon. Hence the Chaldeans and Syrians even today call the festival *'id*

Sham'oun al-Shaikh (Feast of Simeon the Old Man). In the Western Church the commemoration of this event appeared first in the liturgical books (*Gelasianum, Gregorianum*) of the seventh and eighth centuries. It bore the title "Purification of Mary" and was listed for February 2 (forty days after Christmas). It has often been said that the feast was introduced in Rome to replace by a liturgical procession the pagan torch parades of the Lupercalia, which had been held in ancient Rome on February 15. Such explanations, however, are judged erroneous by modern scholars, for the festival was never kept on February 15 in the Western Church; moreover, there was no procession of lights in the beginning, and the pagan custom of the Lupercalia had long been discontinued by the time the procession was inaugurated. As a matter of fact, over three hundred years intervened between the last parade of the Lupercalia and the first procession of Candlemas.[45]

It was Pope Sergius I (701) who prescribed the procession with candles, not only for the Feast of the Purification but also for the other three feasts of Mary which were then annually celebrated in Rome (Annunciation, Assumption, Nativity of Mary). The procession was first instituted as a penitentiary rite with prayers (*litaniae*) imploring God's mercy; hence the Church uses the penitential color (purple) even now for the blessing of candles and for the procession.

The original rite of Pope Sergius did not provide for

any blessing of candles. The celebrant in those early centuries distributed to the clergy, for the procession, candles that were neither blessed nor lighted. The ceremony of blessing originated at the end of the eighth century in the Carolingian Empire, as did most of the other liturgical blessings (Easter fire, Easter water, palms, etc.).

In present liturgical usage the officiating priest blesses the candles before the Mass. He sings or recites five prayers of blessing, two of which are given here in English translation:

O holy Lord, almighty Father, eternal God, thou hast created all things from nothing; thou hast commanded the bees to produce this liquid of wax which has been made into a perfect candle; thou hast on this day fulfilled the petitions of the just Simeon: We humbly implore thee through the invocation of thy holy name and through the intercession of Mary, ever Virgin, whose feast we devoutly celebrate today, also through the prayers of all thy saints: Deign to bless and sanctify these candles for human use, for the welfare of body and soul both on land and on water. These thy servants desire to carry them in their hands while they praise thee with their hymns: Hear their voices graciously from thy holy Heaven and from the throne of thy majesty; be merciful to all who cry to thee, whom thou hast redeemed by the precious blood of thy Son, who lives and reigns with thee, God for ever and ever. Amen.

Lord Jesus Christ, true light that enlightens every man who comes into this world, bestow thy blessing upon these candles, and sanctify them with the light of thy grace. As these tapers burn with visible fire and dispel the darkness of night, so may our hearts with the help of thy grace be enlightened by the invisible fire of the splendor of the Holy Ghost, and may be free from all blindness of sin. Clarify the eyes of our minds that we may see what is pleasing to thee and conducive to our salvation. After the dark perils of this life let us be worthy to reach the eternal light. Through thee, Jesus Christ, Savior of the world, who in perfect Trinity livest and reignest, God, for ever and ever. Amen.[46]

After the blessing the celebrant distributes the candles to the clergy and faithful, who carry them in their hands during the solemn procession. Meanwhile the choir sings the canticle of Simeon, *Nunc Dimittis* (Luke 2, 29-32), and various antiphons. The symbolism of the light procession is obvious from the antiphon that is repeated after every verse of the canticle, *Lumen ad revelationem gentium* (a light of revelation to the gentiles). It represents Christ, the Light of the World, at His presentation in the temple of Jerusalem.

From the blessing of candles and the procession of lights come the names of the feast in most countries: Candlemas (English), *Lichtmess* (German), *Candelas* (Spanish), *Candelora* (Italian), *Chandeleur* (French), *Hromnice* (Feast of Candles among the Slovaks and Czechs), *Svijetlo Marijino* (Light Feast of Mary in Yugoslavia). The Slavs of the Eastern Rite (Russians,

Ukrainians) call it "Meeting of the Lord" (*Stretenije Gospoda*).

The procession is always held on February 2, even when the Mass and Office are transferred to another day. In most places it is now held inside the church, but in past centuries the clergy used to proceed into the open and walk through the churchyard past the graves of departed parishioners.

During medieval times the custom developed in Rome of the pope distributing blessed candles after the services from a window of his palace. Naturally, many incidents and accidents occurred. People pressed and pushed each other, quarrels and fighting ensued, and sometimes a person was trampled to death. Pope Gregory XIII abolished the ceremony in 1573 because of these abuses. In its place there appeared another custom at the end of the eighteenth century: representatives of the clergy and laity of Rome offer large and beautifully decorated candles to the Holy Father every year on February 2. The pope receives the candles in the hall of the Consistory, and afterward distributes them to poor churches in his diocese.

In some countries the faithful use large and adorned candles, which they bring along for the blessing. Among the Syrians and Chaldeans the sexton of the parish church prepares these candles, which are made of unbleached wax and painted with designs of gold. In central and eastern Europe people bring candles and tapers of various colors, decorated with flower motifs, holy pictures, and liturgical symbols. After the blessing they take them home and keep them all through the year as cherished sacramentals, to be lighted during storms and lightning, in sickrooms, and at the bedside of dying persons.

The Poles have a beautiful legend that Mary, the "Mother of God of the Blessed Thunder Candle" (*Matka Boska Gromniczna*) watches on wintry nights around Candlemas, when hungry wolves are on rampage outside the sleeping village. With her thunder candle she wards off the ravenous pack and protects the peasants from all harm.

In ancient times the tenant farmers had to pay their rent at Candlemas. After this disagreeable task they were entertained by the landlord with a sumptuous banquet. Candlemas is also the term day for rural laborers in most countries of central Europe and in England. Both farm hands and maids who have hired themselves out for the coming season move in with their new masters and begin work on February 3.

All over Europe Candlemas was considered one of the great days of weather forecasting. Popular belief claims that bad weather and cloudy skies on February 2 mean an early and prosperous summer. If the sun shines through the greater part of Candlemas Day, there will be at least forty more days of cold and snow. This superstition is familiar to all in our famous story of the ground hog looking for his shadow on Candlemas Day.

In rural sections of Austria it is held an omen of blessing and good luck if the sun breaks through the cloudy skies just for a few minutes to cast its radiant glow over the earth. Children wait for this moment and greet the appearance of the sunlight with little songs like this one from the province of Vorarlberg:

> Hail, glorious herald, holy light,
> God sends you from His Heaven bright.
> Your cheerful glow and golden rays
> May bring us happy summer days.
> Lead us through earthly toil and strife
> To everlasting light and life.

Finally, Candlemas Day used to be, and still is in many countries, the end of the popular Christmas season. Cribs and decorations are taken down with care and stored away for the following Christmas season. The Christmas plants are burned, together with the remnants of the Yule log, and the ashes are strewn over garden and fields to insure wholesome and healthy growth for the coming spring.[47]

LITURGICAL PRAYER: *Almighty and eternal God, we humbly beseech Thy majesty: as Thy only-begotten Son was presented in the temple this day in the substance of our flesh, so let us be presented unto Thee with cleansed souls.*

CHAPTER 8

The Annunciation

This feast, which commemorates the message of the Angel Gabriel to Mary and the Incarnation of Christ (Luke 1, 26-38), bears the official title "Annunciation of the Blessed Virgin Mary." In early medieval times it was called the "Annunciation of the Lord" or the "Conception of Christ," indicating that in those days it was considered more a festival of the Lord. Its date, March 25, is placed nine months before the celebration of Christ's birth (Christmas).

The feast was held in the Eastern Church as early as the fifth century. It was introduced into the West during the sixth and seventh centuries. The Tenth Synod of Toledo (656) mentions it as a festival already well known and universally celebrated. It was kept on

94

the same date as in the East, March 25. In many churches of Spain, however, it was annually held on December 18. During the eleventh century the Spaniards adopted the Roman date but also retained their own, so they had two feasts in honor of the Annunciation. In the eighteenth century Rome replaced the Annunciation in December with a feast of the "Expectation of Birth of the Blessed Virgin" (meaning that Mary expected the birth of Christ). The Gospel of the new feast is still that of the Annunciation.

The name of the feast in most nations is the same as the liturgical one, either in its Latin form or in translation, like *Verkündigung* in German. In the Greek Church it is called *Evangelismos* (Glad Tidings), among the Slavs of the Eastern Rite, *Blagovescenije Marii* (Glad Tidings of Mary). The Slavs of the Latin Rite call it *Zvestovanie Panie Marii* (Message to Lady Mary), the Arabic Christians *'id al-bishara* (Feast of Good News).

A popular name in central Europe is "Feast of Swallows" (*Schwalbentag, Fecskek napja*). It is the general belief (and usually happens) that the first swallows return from their migration on or about this day. An ancient saying in Austria claims:

> When Gabriel does the message bring,
> Return the swallows, comes the spring.

This coincidence might have been the reason why people in medieval Europe ascribed to the swallows a certain hallowed character They call them "God's birds" in Hungary, "Mary's birds" in Austria and Germany; and no farmer would ever kill swallows or destroy their nests. Another reason might well have been the fact (made known in Europe by Crusaders and pilgrims) that the town of Nazareth, where the Annunciation took place, has an abundance of swallows circling the houses all day with their cheerful twittering.

The Annunciation was a feast of obligation and one of the public holydays in the Middle Ages. In Catholic countries it was so celebrated up to 1918 when the obligation of attending Mass and resting from work was rescinded by the new Code of Canon Law. In the liturgy, however, it still enjoys its character as one of the major feasts of Mary.

In the early Christian centuries March 25 was observed in a special way as the Day of the Incarnation. In order to make the Lord's life on earth an exact number of years, even down to the day, an early tradition claimed that it was also the date of the crucifixion. This fact is mentioned in many ancient martyrologies (calendars of feasts) and in the sermons of various Fathers of the Church. Soon other events of the history of our salvation were placed on this day by legendary belief, and thus we find in some calendars of the Middle Ages the following quaint "anniversaries" listed for March 25:

> The Creation of the World
> The Fall of Adam and Eve

The Sacrifice of Isaac
The Exodus of the Jews from Egypt
The Incarnation
The Crucifixion and Death of Christ
The Last Judgment [48]

It was an ancient custom of the papal *Curia* (executive office) to start the year on March 25 in all their communications and documents, thus calling it the "Year of the Incarnation." This practice was also adopted by most civil governments for the legal dating of documents. In fact, the Feast of the Annunciation, called "Lady Day," marked the beginning of the legal year in England even after the Reformation, up to 1752.

The scene of the Annunciation used to be represented in mystery plays. In the cathedrals of France, Italy, Germany, and England, on the feast itself, or on a Wednesday in Lent, the "Golden Mass" (*Missa Aurea*) was celebrated, during which the Blessed Virgin and Gabriel were represented by deacons kneeling in the sanctuary and singing the Gospel of the Mass in Latin dialogue, while another deacon sang the part of the narrator. It is reported that the Golden Mass was inaugurated at Tournay in Belgium in 1231.[49]

In other places the solemn Mass was followed by a procession in which a choir boy representing Mary was led through the church and the churchyard. In western Germany, a boy dressed as an angel and suspended

97

on a rope from the Holy Ghost Hole would slowly descend inside the church and, hanging in midair, would address "Mary" with the words of Gabriel. While the children stared up at the approaching "angel" their mothers put cookies and candy on the pew benches, making their little ones believe that Gabriel's invisible companion angels had brought them these presents from Heaven.[50]

In the city of Rome a colorful and splendid procession used to be held on the feast day at the end of the Middle Ages. A richly decorated carriage bearing a picture of the Blessed Virgin was drawn by six black horses from Saint Peter's to Santa Maria della Minerva. There the pope celebrated a pontifical Mass and afterward distributed fifty gold pieces to each of three hundred deserving poor girls to provide them with the necessary means for an honorable and appropriate marriage.

In Russia priests would bless large wafers of wheat flour and present them to the faithful after the service. Returning home, the father would hand a small piece of the wafer to each member of his family and to the servants. They received it with a deep bow and ate it in silence. Later on in the day they took the remaining crumbs of the "Annunciation bread" out into the fields and buried them in the ground as a protection against blight, hail, frost, and drought.

In central Europe the farmers put a picture representing the Annunciation in the barrel that holds the seed grain. While doing so they pronounce some ancient prayer rhyme like this one from upper Austria:

> O Mary, Mother, we pray to you;
> Your life today with fruit was blessed:
> Give us the happy promise, too,
> That our harvest will be of the best.
> If you protect and bless the field,
> A hundredfold each grain must yield.

Having thus implored the help of Mary, they start sowing their summer grains on the following day, assured that no inclement weather will threaten their crops, for, as the ancient saying goes,

> Saint Gabriel to Mary flies:
> This is the end of snow and ice.

LITURGICAL PRAYER: *O God, who didst will that Thy Word take flesh in the womb of the blessed Virgin Mary at the message of the angel: grant us, we pray, to be aided before Thee by her intercession, whom we believe to be truly the Mother of God.*

CHAPTER 9

The Assumption

This feast, celebrated on August 15, is the oldest of all the festivals of Mary. It has not only kept its character as a holyday of obligation up to now but has been brought into even greater significance through the solemn declaration in 1950 of the dogma of Mary's assumption into Heaven.

The first annual feast day of Mary seems to have been celebrated in Palestine. In a eulogy on Saint Theodosius (529), Bishop Theodore of Petra wrote that the monks of Palestine held every year with great solemnity and devotion a memorial feast of the Blessed Virgin (*Theotokou Mneme:* the Memory of the Mother of God). Neither the occasion nor the date of this "memory" is mentioned, but there is little doubt that it was a celebration on the anniversary of her "falling asleep." According to ancient tradition the date was August 15.

This annual commemoration of Mary soon spread throughout the whole Eastern Church. Emperor Mauritius in 602 confirmed the date and established the feast as a public holiday for his entire realm. Its official title was the "Falling Asleep of the Mother of God" (*Koinesis Theotokou*). Almost immediately Rome accepted this festival and celebrated it in the seventh century under the same title (*Dormitio Beatae Mariae Virginis*).

With the memory of Mary's "falling asleep," however, there was everywhere connected the ancient traditional belief that her body did not decay but soon after the burial was united again with her soul by the miraculous action of Divine Omnipotence, and was taken up to Heaven. In the Latin Church this general belief brought about a change in the title of the feast. Very soon, in the seventh and eighth centuries, it started to be called *Assumptio* (Taking Up).

The universal belief of Mary's assumption has been framed in ancient legends and stories which, though not strictly historical in themselves, confirm the underlying tradition. The most famous of these legends is quoted in an interpolated passage (added by an unknown author) in the sermons of Saint John Damascene (749). It tells how the East Roman Emperor Marcian (457) and his wife, Pulcheria, asked the

Bishop of Jerusalem at the Council of Chalcedon, in 451, to have the relics of the Blessed Virgin brought to Constantinople. The Bishop is said to have answered, "Mary died in the presence of the Apostles; but her tomb, when opened later on the request of Saint Thomas, was found empty, and thus the Apostles concluded that the body was taken up to Heaven." [51]

Although the above legend was not actually told by Saint John Damascene, in one of his sermons he clearly expressed the same general belief of all Christianity:

Your sacred and happy soul, as nature will have it, was separated in death from your most blessed and immaculate body; and although the body was duly interred, it did not remain in the state of death, neither was it dissolved by decay. . . . Your most pure and sinless body was not left on earth but you were transferred to your heavenly throne, o Lady, Queen, and Mother of God in truth. [52]

It is this fact of Mary's assumption into Heaven that has been formally celebrated from the beginning of the Middle Ages in all Christian countries up to the Reformation, and in the Catholic Church up to this day. The other two events connected with it, her "falling asleep" and her coronation in Heaven, are included in the feast but not expressly commemorated. In South America, however, a special feast of Mary's coronation is held annually on August 18.

When Pope Pius XII, on November 1, 1950, solemnly announced the Assumption of Mary to be a dogma of the faith, he did not establish a new doctrine but merely confirmed the universal belief of early Christianity, declaring it to be revealed by God through the medium of Apostolic tradition. He also introduced a new Mass text which more clearly stresses the fact of the Assumption in its prayers and readings.

The feast was given a vigil and liturgical octave by Pope Leo IV in 874. The octave, however, was abolished in 1955, together with the octaves of all feasts except Christmas, Easter, and Pentecost. The Council of Mainz in 813 prescribed the celebration for the whole empire of the West as a public holyday. Soon after, the popes extended this obligation to the entire Latin Church.

In the Greek Rite the official title of the feast is still the ancient one (Falling Asleep): *Koinesis Theotokou* in Greek, *Uspenije Marii* in Slavonic. Most European nations have adopted the Latin term of *Assumptio*, like Assumption in English, *Assunción* in Spanish, *Assomption* in French. The German *Mariä Himmelfahrt* means "Mary's Going Up to Heaven," as does the South Slavic *Usnesenje* and the North Slavic *Nanebovzatie*. Among the Syrians and Chaldeans the feast is called *'id al-intiqal Marjam* (The Being Transferred of Mary).

Among the Hungarians the Assumption is kept with special solemnity as a great national holiday. According to legend their first king, Saint Stephen (1038), offered the sacred royal crown to Mary, thereby choosing her as the heavenly Queen and Patroness of the whole country. Consequently, they call it the "Feast of Our Great Lady" (*Nagyboldogasszonynap*), and Mary is referred to as the "Great Lady of the Hungarians" (*Magna Domina Hungarorum*). They observe August 15 with unusual solemnities, pageants, parades, and universal rejoicing.

In France a traditional pageant used to be performed in many places on Assumption Day. Figures of angels descended within the church to a flowery "sepulchre" and reascended again with an image of the Blessed Virgin dazzlingly robed, while boys dressed as angels played with wooden mallets on a musical keyboard the tune of a popular Madonna hymn.

The Armenians list the Feast of the Assumption among the five supreme festivals (*Daghavár*) of the year. As such it is preceded by a whole week of fasting and consists of a three-day celebration of which the second day is the actual feast of obligation. It is also followed by a solemn liturgical octave.

In pre-Christian times the season from the middle of August to the middle of September was observed as a period of rejoicing and thanksgiving for the successful harvest of grains. Many symbolic rites were aimed toward assuring man of prosperous weather for the reaping of the fall fruits and for winter planting. Some elements of these ancient cults are now connected with the feast and season of the Assumption. All through the Middle Ages the days from August 15 to September 15 were called "Our Lady's Thirty Days" (*Frauendreissiger*) in the German-speaking sections of Europe. Many Assumption shrines even today show Mary clothed in a robe covered with ears of grain. These images (*Maria im Gerteidekleid,* Our Lady of Grains) are favored goals of pilgrimages during August.

Popular legends ascribe a character of blessing and goodness to Our Lady's Thirty Days. Both animals and plants are said to lose their harmful traits. Poisonous snakes do not strike, poison plants are harmless, wild animals refrain from attacking humans. All food produced during this period is especially wholesome and good, and will remain fresh much longer than at other times of the year.

The fact that herbs picked in August were considered of great power in healing occasioned the medieval practice of the "Blessing of Herbs" on Assumption Day. The Church thus elevated a popular belief of pre-Christian times into an observance of religious import and gave it the character of a Christian rite of deep and appropriate meaning. In central Europe the feast itself was called "Our Lady's Herb Day" (*Kräutertag* in German, *Matka Boska Zielna* in Polish). In the Alpine provinces the blessing of herbs is still bestowed before the solemn service of the Assumption. The city of Würzburg in Bavaria used to be a favored center of these blessings, and from this fact it seems to have received its very name in the twelfth century (*Würz:* spice herb).[53] The Roman Ritual still provides an official blessing of herbs on Assumption Day which, among other prayers, contains the petition that God may bless the medicinal powers of these herbs and make them mercifully efficient against diseases and poisons in humans and domestic animals.[54]

The Eastern Rites have similar blessings. In fact, the Syrians celebrate a special feast of "Our Lady of Herbs" on May 15. Among the Armenians, the faithful bring the first grapes from their vineyards to church on Assumption Day to have them solemnly blessed by the priest. Before breakfast the father distributes them to his family. No one would dream of tasting the new harvest before consuming the first blessed grapes on Our Lady's Day.

In Sicily people keep a partial or total abstinence from fruit during the first two weeks of August (*La Quindicina*) in honor of the Blessed Virgin. On the feast day itself they have all kinds of fruit blessed in church and serve them at dinner. They also present each other with baskets of fruit on Assumption Day.

From early centuries the Feast of the Assumption was a day of great religious processions. This popular custom seems to have started with the ancient Roman practice, which Pope Sergius I (701) inaugurated, of having liturgical prayer-processions (*litaniae*) on the major feasts of Mary. In many places of central Europe, also in Spain, France, Italy, and South America, such processions are held. In Austria the faithful, led by the priest, walk through the fields and meadows imploring God's blessing upon the harvest with prayer and hymns.

In France, where Mary under the title of her Assumption is the primary patron of the country, her statue is carried in solemn procession through the cities and towns on August 15, with great splendor and pageantry, while church bells peal and the faithful sing hymns in Mary's honor.

The Italian people, too, are fond of solemn processions on August 15, a custom which is also practiced among the Italian-Americans in the United States. In the rural sections outside Rome the so-called "Bowing Procession" (*L'Inchinata*) is held, the statue of Mary being carried through the town (symbolizing her journey to Heaven). Under a gaily decorated arch of branches and flowers (representing the gate of Heaven) it is met by a statue of Christ. Both images are inclined toward each other three times as though they were solemnly bowing. Then "Christ" conducts his "mother" back to the parish church (symbolizing her entrance into eternal glory), where the ceremony is concluded with a service of solemn benediction.

In Sardinia the procession is called *Candelieri* because they carry seven immense candlesticks each supporting a torch of a hundred pounds of wax. The procession goes to the Church of the Assumption where the candles are placed beside Mary's shrine. The origin of the *Candelieri* dates back to the year 1580 when a deadly epidemic suddenly stopped on August 15 after the town had vowed to honor Mary by offering these candles every year.

It may be of interest to note that on the island of Sardinia, according to ancient tradition, all shrines of the Assumption picture Mary not as being assumed into Heaven but as reclining on her bed. Thus they perpetuate the original commemoration of the feast, the "falling asleep" of the Blessed Virgin.

Finally, there is the old and inspiring custom on August 15 of blessing the elements of nature which are the scene of man's labors and the source of human food. In all Christian countries before the Reformation the clergy used to bless the countryside, its farms, orchards, fields, and gardens. In the western sections of Austria the priests still perform the "Blessing of the Alps," including not only the mountains and meadows but also the farms.

In the Alpine sections of France the parish priests ride from pasture to pasture on Assumption Day or during the octave. Behind the priest on the horse sits an acolyte holding the holy water vessel. At every meadow the blessing is given to the animals which are gathered around a large cross decorated with branches and flowers.

In the Latin countries, especially in Portugal, the ocean and the fishermen's boats are blessed on the afternoon of Assumption Day. This custom has also come to the United States, where fishing fleets and ocean are now solemnly blessed in various coastal towns on August 15.

LITURGICAL PRAYER: *Almighty and eternal God, who hast taken up into the glory of Heaven, with body and soul, the Immaculate Virgin Mary, Mother of Thy Son: grant us, we pray, that we may always strive after heavenly things and thus merit to share in her glory.*

CHAPTER 10

The Nativity of Mary

A feast in honor of Mary's birth seems to have been held in Syria and Palestine in the sixth century. Saint Romanus (457), a native of Syria and later deacon of a church in Constantinople, was probably the first one who brought this feast to the attention of the authorities of the Greek Church. He wrote a hymn in honor of Mary's birth and spread the knowledge of this festival among the population of East Rome. His efforts were highly successful, for in the following centuries mention is made of a celebration of Mary's nativity in many churches of the empire. Saint Andrew of Crete (740), Archbishop, preached sermons in honor of the feast, as did Saint John Damascene.

This celebration was accepted and adopted by

the Roman Church at the end of the seventh century. It spread very slowly through the rest of Europe. Saint Fulbert (1028), Bishop of Chartres, mentioned it in one of his sermons as a "recent" feast. By the twelfth century, however, it was observed among all Christian nations as one of the major feasts of Mary, and remained a holyday of obligation until 1918.

There is no historical evidence to indicate why the Nativity of Mary should fall precisely on September 8. As usual in such cases, legends of a later period supply the missing motivation by miraculous events. There is a lovely medieval legend giving the reason for the date: The feast was made September 8 because in the fifth century a pious farmer at Angers in France one night had a vision of angels singing in Heaven. When he inquired for the reason he was told that they were rejoicing because the Blessed Virgin was born that night. It happened to be September 8. So the good farmer went to the Bishop, Saint Maurilius (430), who, after convincing himself of the farmer's sincerity, established a feast in honor of the birth of Mary to be celebrated annually on that day.

Actually, of course, the festival did not originate in France but came from the Middle East. The real reason for the date is unknown. It is not improbable, though, that a genuine ancient tradition of the Church in Jerusalem provided the date, especially since the feast originated in Palestine; and all the Eastern Churches have celebrated Mary's nativity either on

September 8 or 9 from the earliest times. The Syrians observe on this day also the solemn memory of the parents of Mary, Saint Joachim and Saint Anna.

In many places of central and eastern Europe the Feast of Mary's Nativity is traditionally connected with ancient thanksgiving customs and celebrations. The day itself marks the end of the summer in popular reckoning, the beginning of the Indian summer, which is called "after-summer" (*Nachsommer*), and the start of the fall planting season. A blessing of the harvest and of the seed grains for the winter crops is performed in many churches. The formula of this blessing may be found in the Roman Ritual.[55]

In the wine-growing sections of France, September 8 is the day of the grape harvest festival. The owners of vineyards bring their best grapes to church to have them blessed, and afterward tie some of them to the hands of the statue of the Virgin. The Feast of Mary's Nativity is called "Our Lady of the Grape Harvest" in those sections, and a festive meal is held at which the first grapes of the new harvest are consumed.

In the Alps the "down-driving" (*Abtrieb*) begins on September 8. Cattle and sheep leave their summer pastures on the high mountain slopes where they have roamed for months, and descend in long caravans to the valleys to take up their winter quarters in the warm stables. The lead animals wear elaborate decorations of flowers and ribbons; the rest carry branches of evergreen between their horns and little bells around their necks. The shepherds and caretakers (*Sennen*) accompany the caravan, dressed in all their finery and decorated with Alpine flowers, singing their ancient songs, yodeling, and cracking whips to provoke a multiple echo from the surrounding mountain cliffs. Arriving at the bottom of the valley in the evening, they find the whole village or town awaiting them in a festive mood. Ample fodder is served to the cattle in the stables, and a banquet unites the family and farm hands in each house.

If, however, the farmer who owns the cattle or one of the *Sennen* has died during the summer, the "down-driving" is performed without decorations and in silence. Each animal then wears a mourning wreath of purple or black crepe. In some sections of Austria all the milk obtained on Drive-Down Day is given to the poor in honor of our Lady, together with the meat, bread, and pastries left over from the feast in the evening.

In central and northern Europe, according to ancient belief, September 8 is also the day on which the swallows leave for the sunny skies of the South. A popular children's rhyme in Austria contains the following lines:

> It's Blessed Virgin's Birthday,
> The swallows do depart;
> Far to the South they fly away,
> And sadness fills my heart.
> But after snow and ice and rain
> They will in March return again.

113

LITURGICAL PRAYER: *We pray Thee, O Lord, grant to Thy servants the gift of heavenly grace: as the childbearing of the blessed Virgin was the beginning of our salvation, so may the devout celebration of her Nativity accord us an increase of peace.*

CHAPTER 11

The Immaculate Conception

This is the only one of the Blessed Virgin's festivals that did not come to the Western Church by way of Rome but spread from the Byzantine province of southern Italy first into Normandy, thence to England, France, and Germany, until it was finally accepted into the Roman liturgy and approved for the whole Latin Church.

Like the other feasts of Mary, it had its origin in the Eastern Church. There it was introduced in various local churches during the eighth century. It bore the title the "Conception [*Syllepsis*] of the Mother of God." More frequently, however, it was called the "Conception of Saint Anne" (meaning that Saint Anne conceived Mary). The feast spread gradually over the Eastern Empire until Emperor Manuel Comnenus in 1166 recognized it as a public festival and prescribed it as a holiday for the entire Byzantine realm.

The conception of no other saint was ever commemorated by the Church. The reason why Mary was accorded this exceptional honor lies in the general belief of Christianity that she was free from original sin because of her dignity as mother of God. This belief is found in many testimonies from the earliest centuries. It is clearly stated in the famous "Letter of the Priests and Deacons of Achaja" on the martyrdom of Saint Andrew (first century).[56] Many scholars do not consider this document genuine; however, it could not have been written later than the end of the fourth century, because its text is used in the earliest missals of the Gothic clergy. Thus the letter, whether genuine or not, by its very antiquity proves the belief of early Christians in the Immaculate Conception—in the fact that Mary was free from original sin.

From Constantinople this festival came to Naples in the ninth century, for Naples was then a part of the East Roman Empire. It was celebrated in Sicily, Naples, and lower Italy under the name "Conception of Saint Anne." When the Normans conquered those Byzantine provinces in the eleventh century, they adopted the feast and brought it back to Normandy, where it soon became established as a beloved annual celebration. Through Norman influence it came into England in the twelfth century and into various dioceses of France and Germany during the twelfth to fourteenth centuries. The fact that the Normans had brought it into western Europe is indicated by the popular name which it bore in medieval times, "Feast of the Normans."

While the feast thus slowly spread in western Europe, Rome neither celebrated nor officially recommended it but allowed it to be introduced wherever the local church authorities wished to establish it. Saint Thomas Aquinas mentions this in his famous *Summa Theologiae:* "Although the Roman Church does not celebrate it, she allows other churches to do so." [57] It was precisely for this reason that many bishops and theologians opposed it as an "innovation." Its fate was also intimately connected with the theological disputations that went on for centuries among the learned as to whether Mary was entirely free from original sin even "at the first moment" of her conception.

Meanwhile, the observance of the feast proceeded on its victorious course. The Franciscans made themselves fervent promoters of its celebration. They were soon joined by the Benedictines, Cistercians, and Carmelites. In the religious houses of these orders, both in Rome and elsewhere, the feast was annually kept with great solemnity. By the end of the fourteenth

117

century it was well established in most European countries.

Finally, in 1477, Pope Sixtus IV officially acknowledged the feast and allowed its celebration in the whole Church without, however, commanding it. It was not until the eighteenth century that Pope Clement XI (1721) prescribed it as an annual feast to be celebrated on December 8 (but not yet as a holyday of obligation). In Spain, though, it has been kept as a public holyday since 1644.

The festival obtained its present high rank in 1854, when Pope Pius IX solemnly declared the dogma of the Immaculate Conception of Mary and at the same time raised its commemoration to the status of a holyday of obligation for the universal Church. A new Mass and office were introduced, and the term "Immaculate Conception" was officially incorporated in the liturgical books. The churches of the Greek Rite have kept the festival as a prescribed holyday since 1166, though they still use the ancient title, "Conception of Saint Anne."

The dogma of the Immaculate Conception confirmed and clarified with finality the overwhelming conviction of the entire Christian world before the Reformation that Mary, through a special privilege of God, was free from original sin even at the first moment of her conception. The Pope's official and solemn declaration was received with immense joy by the faithful all over the world; and the great festival commemorating this sacred event is now annually observed as one of the two highest ranking feasts of Mary in all Catholic churches.

Because of its very recent establishment as a holyday of obligation, this feast has not developed any popular customs and traditions except in Spain and Spanish-speaking countries, where it has been a great public feast day for the past three hundred years.

Since Mary, under the title of the Immaculate Conception, is the primary patron of Spain, her feast is celebrated everywhere with great public solemnity. People prepare themselves by novenas and nocturnal vigils for the feast, solemn processions with the statue of the Immaculate are made after High Mass, and additional services are held in the afternoon of the holyday. In many places December 8 is also the day for the solemn first communion of children.

In the northern provinces of Spain it is the custom to decorate the balconies of the houses with flowers, carpets, and flags on the eve of the feast, and candles burn in the windows all through the night. In Seville, the famous "Dance of the Six" (*Los Seises*) is performed in the cathedral on the feast day and during the octave. Six boys, their heads covered according to special privilege, enact an ancient religious pageant before the Blessed Sacrament, dancing in the sanctuary and singing hymns in honor of the Immaculate Conception. This performance annually draws large crowds of devout natives and curious tourists.

119

All through Spain December 8 is the traditional day of great school celebrations. Alumni revisit their alma mater and spend the day in joyful reunion with their classmates and former teachers. In many countries of South America it is the day of commencement celebrations, since the long summer vacations start around the middle of December.

Mary Immaculate is also the patroness of the Spanish infantry and civil guard (state police). On December 8 in all towns and cities, troops attend Mass in a body. It is a colorful pageant to watch. Detachments in splendid uniforms march with military precision, brass bands play ancient, stirring music, and the picture of the Immaculate Conception on each regimental flag is held aloft.

Finally, there is the interesting fact that our modern custom of an annual "Mothers' Day" has been associated in Spain with the Feast of the Immaculate Conception. All over Spain December 8 is Mothers' Day, and thus the great feast of our Lady has also become an outstanding day of joyful family celebrations in honor of mothers everywhere in that country.

LITURGICAL PRAYER: *O God who, through the Immaculate Conception of the Virgin, didst prepare a worthy habitation for Thy Son: grant us, we pray, as by the foreseen death of Thy Son thou didst preserve her from all stain of sin, so we may be cleansed by her intercession and may come to Thee.*

CHAPTER 12

All Saints and All Souls

All Saints · The Church of Antioch kept a commemoration of all holy martyrs on the first Sunday after Pentecost. Saint John Chrysostom, who served as preacher at Antioch before he became Patriarch of Constantinople, delivered annual sermons on the occasion of this festival. They were entitled "Praise of All the Holy Martyrs of the Entire World." [58] In the course of the succeeding centuries the feast spread through the whole Eastern Church and, by the seventh century, was everywhere kept as a public holyday.

In the West the Feast of "All Holy Martyrs" was introduced when Pope Boniface IV (615) was given the ancient Roman temple of the Pantheon by Emperor Phocas (610) and dedicated it as a church to the

Blessed Virgin Mary and all the martyrs. The date of this dedication was May 13, and on this date the feast was then annually held in Rome. Two hundred years later Pope Gregory IV (844) transferred the celebration to November 1. The reason for this transfer is quite interesting, especially since some scholars have claimed that the Church assigned All Saints to November 1 in order to substitute a feast of Christian significance for the pagan Germanic celebrations of the demon cult at that time of the year. Actually, the reason for the transfer was that the many pilgrims who came to Rome for the "Feast of the Pantheon" could be fed more easily after the harvest than in the spring.[59]

Meanwhile, the practice had spread of including in this memorial not only all martyrs but the other saints as well. Pope Gregory III (741) had already stated this when he dedicated a chapel in Saint Peter's in honor of Christ, Mary, and "all the apostles, martyrs, confessors, and all the just and perfect servants of God whose bodies rest throughout the whole world." [60]

Upon the request of Pope Gregory IV, Emperor Louis the Pious (840) introduced the Feast of All Saints in his territories. With the consent of the bishops of Germany and France he ordered it to be kept on November 1 in the whole empire. Finally, Pope Sixtus IV (1484) established it as a holyday of obligation for the entire Latin Church, giving it a liturgical vigil and octave.

122

The purpose of the feast is twofold. As the prayer of the Mass states, "the merits of all the saints are venerated in common by this one celebration," because a very large number of martyrs and other saints could not be accorded the honor of a special festival since the days of the year would not suffice for all these individual celebrations. The second purpose was given by Pope Urban IV: Any negligence, omission, and irreverence committed in the celebration of the saints' feasts throughout the year is to be atoned for by the faithful, and thus due honor may still be offered to these saints.[61]

LITURGICAL PRAYER: *Almighty and eternal God, who hast granted us to venerate the merits of all Thy saints in one celebration: we beg Thee to bestow upon us the desired abundance of Thy mercy on account of this great number of intercessors.*

All Souls · The need and duty of prayer for the departed souls has been acknowledged by the Church at all times. It is recommended in the Scriptures of the Old Testament (2 Macch. 12, 46), and found expression not only in public and private prayers but especially in the offering of the Holy Sacrifice for the repose of souls. The customary dates for public services of this kind were, and still are, the day of death and burial, the seventh and thirtieth day after death (Month's Mind Mass), and the anniversary. Except for the funeral Mass, the actual observance of these dates is not made obligatory by the Church but left to the piety of relatives and friends of the deceased.

The memorial feast of all departed ones in a common celebration was inaugurated by Abbot Saint Odilo of Cluny (1048). He issued a decree that all monasteries of the congregation of Cluny were annually to keep November 2 as a "day of all the departed ones" (*Omnium Defunctorum*). On November 1, after vespers, the bell should be tolled and afterward the Office of the Dead be recited; on the next day all priests had to say Mass for the repose of the souls in purgatory.[62]

This observance of the Benedictines of Cluny was soon adopted by other Benedictines, and by the Carthusians. Pope Sylvester II (1003) approved and recommended it. It was some time, though, before the secular clergy introduced it in the various dioceses. From the eleventh to the fourteenth centuries it gradually spread in France, Germany, England, and Spain, until finally, in the fourteenth century, Rome placed the day of the commemoration of all the faithful departed in the official books of the Western Church for November 2 (or November 3 if the second falls on a Sunday).

November 2 was chosen in order that the memory of all the "holy spirits" both of the saints in Heaven and of the souls in purgatory should be celebrated on two successive days, and in this way to express the Christian belief in the "Communion of Saints." Since

124

the Feast of All Saints had already been celebrated on November 1 for centuries, the memory of the departed souls in purgatory was placed on the following day. In the Greek Rite the commemoration of all the faithful departed is held on the Saturday before Sexagesima Sunday, and is called the "Saturday of the Souls" (*Psychosabbaton*). The Armenians celebrate it on Easter Monday, with the solemn Office of the Dead. The Mass, however, is that of the Resurrection. An interesting and moving observance is held in the Syrian-Antiochene Rite where they celebrate on three separate days: on Friday before Septuagesima they commemorate all departed priests; on Friday before Sexagesima, all the faithful departed; and on Friday before Quinquagesima, "all those who died in strange places, away from their parents and friends."

Pope Benedict XV in 1915 allowed all priests to say three Masses on All Souls' Day in order to give increased help to the suffering souls in purgatory. The Church has also granted to all faithful special privileges of gaining indulgences for the holy souls on November 1 and 2. The Office of the Dead is recited by priests and religious communities. In many places the graves in the cemeteries are blessed on the eve or in the morning of All Souls' Day, and a solemn service is usually held in parish churches.

The liturgical color at all services on November 2 is black. The Masses are part of the group called "Requiem" Masses because they start with the words

Requiem aeternam dona eis (Eternal rest grant unto them).

The sequence sung at the solemn Mass on All Souls' Day (and on other occasions) is the famous poem *Dies Irae* (Day of Wrath) written by a thirteenth-century Franciscan. It has been often ascribed to Thomas of Celano (1260), the friend and biographer of Saint Francis of Assisi, though the authorship is not certain.

Traditional Observance · Numerous ancient customs associated with All Saints and All Souls have come down through the centuries and are still observed in many countries. Some are of a strictly religious nature, such as the custom of decorating the graves and praying in the cemeteries. This practice is general in all Catholic countries both in Europe and America. On the afternoon of All Saints' Day or in the morning of All Souls the faithful visit each individual grave of relatives and friends. Sometimes the congregation, led by the priest, walks in procession to the cemetery. There they pray for all the holy souls in front of the cemetery chapel, then the priest recites the liturgical prayers for the dead and blesses the graves with holy water. Afterward the families separate to offer private prayers at the graves of their loved ones.

During the week preceding All Saints crowds of people may be seen in the cemeteries, usually in the evening after work, decorating the graves of their dear ones with flowers, tending the lawn, and spreading fresh white gravel around the tombs. Candles, protected by little glass lanterns, are placed around the graves or at the foot of the tombstones, to be lighted on All Saints' eve and left burning through the night. It is an impressive, unforgettable sight to look upon the hundreds and often thousands of lights quietly burning in the darkness and dreary solitude of a cemetery. People call them "lights of the holy souls" (*Seelenlichter*).

To visit the graves of dear ones on All Souls is considered a duty of such import that many people in Europe will travel from a great distance to their home towns on All Saints' Day in order to perform this obligation of love and piety.

It is an ancient custom in Catholic sections of central Europe to ring the church bells at the approach of dusk on All Saints' Day, to remind the people to pray for the souls in purgatory. When the pealing of these bells is heard, the families gather in one room of their home, extinguish all other lights save the blessed candle (kept from Candlemas Day) which is put on the table. Kneeling around it, they say the rosary for the holy souls. On this occasion, as on all others throughout the year, the boys and men lead the prayer by reciting the first part of the "Hail Mary" while the women respond with the second part:

Hail, Mary, full of grace, the Lord is with thee, blessed art thou among women, and blessed is the fruit of thy womb, Jesus.

Holy Mary, Mother of God, pray for us sinners, now, and at the hour of our death. Amen.

In the rural sections of Brittany four men alternate in tolling the church bell for an hour on All Saints' Day after dark. Four other men go from farm to farm during the night, ringing hand bells and chanting in each place: "Christians awake, pray to God for the souls of the dead, and say the *Pater* and *Ave* for them." From the house comes the reply "Amen" as the people rise for prayer.

In most countries of South America All Souls' Day is a public holiday. In Brazil people flock by the thousands to the cemeteries all morning, light candles and kneel at the graves in prayer. The deep silence of so many persons in the crowded cemetery deeply impresses the stranger. In Puerto Rico, people will walk for miles to the graves of their loved ones. The women often carry vases of flowers and water, for they know they can get no water at the cemetery to keep the flowers fresh. They wear their best clothes as they trudge along in the hot sun. Whole truckloads of people will arrive at the cemetery if the distance is too far to walk. The priest visits each grave and says the prayers for the dead as the mourners walk along with him. Sometimes the ceremony lasts for hours and it is

128

near midnight when the tired pastor visits the last graves.

Among the native population in the Philippines, a novena is held for the holy souls before November 2. In places where the cemetery is close to the town, candles are brought to be burned at the tombs and prayers are said every night. During these nine days the people also prepare their family tombs for the great "Feast of the Souls." Tomb niches and crosses are repainted, hedges trimmed, flowers planted, and all weeds are removed from the graves. On the evening of All Saints' Day young men go from door to door asking for gifts in the form of cookies, candy, pastry, and sing a traditional verse in which they represent holy souls liberated from purgatory and on their way to Heaven:

> *Kung kami po'y lilimusan*
> *Dali dali ninyong bigyan*
> *Baka kami'y masarhan*
> *Sa pinto ng kalanginan.*

> If you will give us friendly alms,
> Please do not make us wait;
> We want to enter Heaven's door
> Before it is too late.

In Poland, and in Polish churches of the United States, the faithful bring to their parish priest on All Souls' Day paper sheets with black borders called *Wypominki* (Naming) on which are written the names

129

of their beloved dead. During the evening devotions in November, and on Sundays, the names are read from the pulpit and prayers are offered for the repose of the souls.

Our pagan forefathers kept several "cult of the dead" rites at various times of the year. One of these periods was the great celebration at the end of the fall and the beginning of winter (around November 1). Together with the practices of nature and demon lore (fires, masquerades, fertility cults, etc.) they also observed the ritual of the dead with many traditional rites. Since All Saints and All Souls happened to be placed within the period of such an ancient festival, some of the pre-Christian traditions became part of our Christian feast and associated with Christian ideas.

There is, for instance, the pre-Christian practice of putting food at the graves or in the homes at such times of the year when the spirits of the dead were believed to roam their familiar earthly places. The beginning of November was one of these times. By offering a meal or some token food to the spirits, people hoped to please them and to avert any possible harm they could do. Hence came the custom of baking special breads in honor of the holy souls and bestowing them on the children and the poor. This custom is widespread in Europe. "All Souls' bread" (*Seelenbrot*) is made and distributed in Germany, Belgium, France, Austria, Spain, Italy, Hungary, and in the Slavic countries.

In some sections of central Europe boys receive on All Souls' Day a cake shaped in the form of a hare, and girls are given one in the shape of a hen (an interesting combination of "spirit bread" and fertility symbols). These figure cakes are baked of the same dough as the festive cakes which the people eat on All Saints' Day and which are a favorite dish all over central Europe. They are made of braided strands of sweet dough and called "All Saints' cakes" (*Heiligenstriezel* in German, *Strucel Swiateczne* in Polish, *Mindszenti Kalácska* in Hungarian). Here is the recipe:

8 cups flour	1 tsp. grated orange rind
2 cups milk	1 tsp. grated lemon rind
4 yeast cakes	½ cup soft butter
8 egg yolks	1 tsp. salt
2 cups sugar	

Dissolve yeast cakes in ½ cup of the milk. Make thin sponge by mixing yeast with rest of milk and 1 cup of flour. Mix thoroughly, sprinkle top lightly with flour and set aside to rise. Add salt to egg yolks, beat until thick and lemon-colored. Add sugar, rinds, and mix with sponge. Add two cups of flour, alternating with the milk, and knead for half-hour.

Add remaining flour and butter and continue to knead until the dough comes away from the hand. Set in warm place to rise until double in bulk. Separate dough into four parts, roll into long strips and braid into loaf. Brush top with lightly beaten egg yolk and sprinkle with poppy seed. Let rise. Bake in 350° oven for one hour.

In western Europe people prepare on All Souls' Day a meal of cooked beans or peas or lentils, called "soul food," which they afterward serve to the poor together with meat and other dishes. In Poland the farmers hold a solemn meal on the evening of All Souls' Day, with empty seats and plates ready for the "souls" of departed relatives. Onto the plates members of the family put parts of the dinner. These portions are not touched by anyone but afterward are given to beggars or poor neighbors. In the Alpine provinces of Austria destitute children and beggars go from house to house, reciting a prayer or singing a hymn for the holy souls, receiving small loaves of the "soul bread" in reward. There, too, people put aside a part of everything that is cooked on All Souls' Day and give meals to the poor. In northern Spain and in Madrid people distribute and eat a special pastry called "Bones of the Holy" (*Huesos de Santo*). In Catalonia All Souls' pastry is called *Panellets* (little breads).

In Hungary the "Day of the Dead" (*Halottak Napja*) is kept with the traditional customs common to all people in central Europe. In addition, they invite orphan children into the family for All Saints' and All Souls' days, serving them generous meals and giving them new clothes and toys. Another endearing practice is the special care people in Hungary bestow on "forgotten" graves which otherwise would stay neglected and unadorned. Taking turns from year to year, the families of a village assume the care of these graves in ad-

132

dition to their own, decorating them, lighting candles, and praying for the souls of those who are buried in them.

In Brittany the farmers visit the graves of their departed relatives on *Jour des morts* (Day of the Dead), kneeling bareheaded at the mound in long and fervent prayer. Then they sprinkle the grave with holy water, and finally, before leaving, pour milk over the grave as a libation "for the holy souls." In every house a generous portion of the dinner is served before an empty seat and afterward given to the hungry.

Many other customs of the ancient cult of the dead have survived as superstitions to this day. The belief that the spirits of the dead return for All Souls' Day is expressed in a great number of legends and traditions. In the rural sections of Poland the charming story is told that at midnight on All Souls' Day a great light may be seen in the parish church; the holy souls of all departed parishioners who are still in purgatory gather there to pray for their release before the very altar where they used to receive the Blessed Sacrament when still alive. Afterward the souls are said to visit the scenes of their earthly life and labors, especially their homes. To welcome them by an external sign the people leave doors and windows open on All Souls' Day.

In the rural sections of Austria the holy souls are said to wander through the forests on All Souls' Day, sighing and praying for their release, but unable to reach the living by external means which would indicate their presence. For this reason, the children are told to pray aloud while going through the open spaces to church and cemetery, so the poor souls will have the great consolation of seeing that their invisible presence is known and their pitiful cries for help are understood and answered.

The Church has not established any season or octave in connection with All Souls. The faithful, however, have introduced an "octave" of their own, devoting the eight days after All Souls to special prayer, penance, and acts of charity. This custom is widespread in central Europe. People call this particular time of the year "Soul Nights" (*Seelennächte*). Every evening the rosary is said for the holy souls within the family while the blessed candle burns. Many go to Mass every morning. A generous portion of the meal is given to the poor each day; and the faithful abstain from dances and other public amusements out of respect for the holy souls. This is a deeply religious practice filled with a genuine spirit of Christian charity which overshadows and elevates the unholy customs of ancient pagan lore.

LITURGICAL PRAYER: *O God, Creator and Redeemer of all the faithful, grant to the souls of Thy servants departed the remission of all their sins, that through our devout prayers they may obtain the pardon which they have always desired.*

Halloween · Unlike the familiar observance of All Souls, Halloween traditions have never been connected with Christian religious celebrations of any kind. Although the name is taken from a great Christian feast (Allhallows' Eve), it has nothing in common with the feast of All Saints and is, instead, a tradition of pre-Christian times that has retained its original character in form and meaning.

Halloween customs are traced back to the ancient Druids. This is attested to by the fact that they are still observed only in those sections of Europe where the population is wholly or partly of Celtic stock. In ancient times around November 1 the burning of fires marked the beginning of winter. Such Halloween fires are kindled in many places even now, especially in Wales and Scotland.[63]

Another, and more important, tradition is the Druidic belief that during the night of November 1 demons, witches, and evil spirits roamed the earth in wild and furious gambols of joy to greet the arrival of "their season"—the long nights and early dark of the winter months. They had their fun with the poor mortals that night, frightening, harming them, and playing all kinds of mean tricks. The only way, it seemed, for scared humans to escape the persecution of the demons was to offer them things they liked, especially dainty food and sweets. Or, in order to escape the fury of these horrible creatures, a human could disguise himself as one of them and join in their roaming. In this way they would

135

take him for one of their own and he would not be bothered. That is what people did in ancient times, and it is in this very form the custom has come down to us, practically unaltered, as our familiar Halloween celebration: the horrible masks of demons and witches, the disguise in strange and unusual gowns, the ghost figures, the frightening gestures and words, the roaming through the streets at night, the pranks played, and finally the threatening demand of a "trick or treat." The pumpkin "ghosts" or jack-o'-lanterns with a burning candle inside may well be a combination of the demon element and the Halloween fire. These pumpkins are found all over central Europe at Halloween, in France, southern Germany, Austria, Switzerland, and the Slavic countries. So is the custom of masquerading and "trick or treat" rhymes, at least in the rural sections where ancient traditions are still observed.

In those countries that once belonged to the Roman Empire there is the custom of eating or giving away fruit, especially apples, on Halloween. It spread to neighboring countries: to Ireland and Scotland from Britain, and to the Slavic countries from Austria. It is probably based upon a celebration of the Roman goddess Pomona to whom gardens and orchards were dedicated. Since the annual feast of Pomona was held on November 1, the relics of that observance became part of our Halloween celebration, for instance the familiar tradition of "ducking" for apples.

CHAPTER 13

Saints of Winter

Stephen (December 26) · The story of this saint can
be found in the Acts of the Apostles (chaps. 6 and 7).
He is usually pictured in deacon's vestments, with a
palm branch, the symbol of martyrdom, in his hand,
and sometimes with a stone in his left hand, to indicate
his death by stoning. Many images show him wearing a
wreath, which is an allusion to his name, for the Greek
word *Stephanos* means "wreath."

From early times this Saint was venerated as patron
of horses. A poem of the tenth century pictures him as
the owner of a horse and dramatically relates how
Christ Himself miraculously cured the animal for His
beloved Disciple. Though there is no historical basis

137

for this association with horses in the life of Saint Stephen, various explanations have been attempted. Some are founded on ancient Germanic ritual celebrations of horse sacrifices at Yuletide. Others use the fact that in medieval times "Twelfth-night" (Christmas to Epiphany) was a time of rest for domestic animals, and horses, as the most useful servants of man, were accorded at the beginning of this fortnight something like a feast day of their own.

It was a general practice among the farmers in Europe to decorate their horses on Stephen's Day, and bring them to the house of God to be blessed by the priest and afterward ridden three times around the church, a custom still observed in many rural sections. Later in the day the whole family takes a gay ride in a wagon or sleigh (St. Stephen's ride). In Sweden, the holy deacon was changed by early legend into the figure of a native saint, a stable boy who is said to have been killed by the pagans in Helsingland. His name—Staffan—reveals the original saint. The "Staffan Riders" parade through the towns of Sweden on December 26, singing their ancient carols in honor of the "Saint of Horses."

Horses' food, mostly hay and oats, is blessed on Stephen's Day. Inspired by pre-Christmas fertility rites people throw kernels of these blessed oats at one another and at their domestic animals as well. In sections of Poland they even toss the oats at the priest after

Mass. Popular legends say this custom is an imitation of stoning, performed in honor of the Saint's martyrdom. The ancient fertility rite, however, can still be clearly recognized in the Polish custom of boys and girls throwing walnuts at each other on Saint Stephen's Day.

In past centuries water and salt were blessed on this day and kept by farmers to be fed to their horses in case of sickness. Women also baked special breads in the form of horseshoes (St. Stephen's horns: *podkovy*) which were eaten on December 26.

In some parts of the British Isles, Saint Stephen's Day is the occasion for boys (the Wren Boys they are called) to go from house to house, one of them carrying a dead wren on a branch decorated with all kinds of gay, streaming ribbons. Stopping in front of each door they sing a song the words of which run something like this:

> God bless the mistress of this house,
> A golden chain around her neck.
> And if she's sick or if she's sore,
> The Lord have mercy on her soul.

After saluting the master, they then sing:

> The wren, the wren, the king of all birds,
> On Saint Stephen's Day was caught in the furze.
> Up with the kettle and down with the pot,
> And give us our answer and let us be gone.

The master of the house then takes a careful look at the bird to make sure it is a wren and not, perchance, a sparrow; and alms are given to the wandering singers.

LITURGICAL PRAYER: *We beseech Thee, O Lord, grant us to imitate what we revere, that we may learn to love also our enemies; for we celebrate his birthday, who knew how to plead even for his persecutors with Thy Son, our Lord Jesus Christ.*

John the Evangelist (December 27) · This favorite Disciple of Christ was Bishop of Ephesus in Asia Minor and died around the year 100. His grave was a goal for many pilgrimages in the early centuries, and countless legends were told about his tomb. People claimed they saw the earth on top of his grave move up and down, indicating his breathing, and believed he did not really die but only slept in the grave. Another legend claimed that his body was taken up to Heaven after he had "slept" in the tomb for some years. All these stories, of course, are traced to the Saint's own report of what Christ said: "If I wish him to remain until I come, what is it to thee?" (John 21, 23), a statement the Apostles even then had misinterpreted to the effect that John would not die.

St. John's Day was a general holyday in medieval times, not only as the third day of Christmas but also in its own right (as the feast of an Apostle). The significant part of the traditional celebration was the

140

blessing and drinking of wine, called the "Love of St. John" (*Johannesminne; Szent János Aldása*) because, according to legend, the Saint once drank a cup of poisoned wine without suffering harm. The prayer of this blessing can be found in the Roman Ritual (Blessing of Wine on the Feast of Saint John the Evangelist). In central Europe people still practice the custom of bringing wine and cider into the church to be blessed. Later, at home, some of it is poured into every barrel in their wine cellars.

People take Saint John's wine with their meals on December 27, expressing the mutual wish: "Drink the love of Saint John." It is also kept in the house throughout the rest of the year. At weddings, bride and bridegroom take some of it when they return from the church. It is also considered a great aid to travelers and drunk before a long journey as a token of protection and safe return. A sip of Saint John's wine is often used as a sacramental for dying people after they have received the sacraments. It is the last earthly drink to strengthen them for their departure from this world.

In the beginning of his Gospel, Saint John proclaims with great beauty of expression that Christ is the Light of the World. For this reason it was, and still is, the custom in many places at Christmas time, when all the lights in the home express this symbolism, to allow children with the name of John or Joan the privilege of lighting the candles on the Advent wreath and the Christmas tree. Even if the name is taken from John

141

the Baptist, the privilege still holds because the Baptist had been the first one to see the light of divinity shining about the Lord at the baptism in the Jordan.

LITURGICAL PRAYER: *Graciously enlighten Thy Church, O Lord, that she may be illumined by the doctrines of Saint John, Thy Apostle and Evangelist, and thus obtain the gifts of eternity.*

Sebastian (January 20) · This Saint died a martyr under Emperor Diocletian in 288. Later legends present him as an officer in the Pretorian guard who, on the Emperor's orders, was executed by a contingent of archers. Found to be still alive after the "execution," however, he was secretly nursed back to health by a Christian matron. This legend would imply that the Numidian archers, known as the best marksmen in the Roman army, purposely directed their arrows at nonvital parts of his body because they liked him and wanted to save his life. Upon his recovery he courageously went to Diocletian and upbraided him for his cruel persecution of Christianity. The enraged Emperor thereupon had him killed with clubs, and his body thrown into the public sewer whence it was recovered by Christians and reverently buried. His relics were transferred to Soisson in France in 826.

He is usually pictured as a young man, stripped of his clothes, tied to a tree, his body pierced by many arrows. From the tenth century on he was widely venerated as one of the great patron saints against pestilence (the others being Saint Rosalie and Saint Roch). Many shrines were erected in his honor in all European countries, and quaint customs developed for invoking his help. People would carry little arrows of tin or silver which had been touched to his relics. An old song of 1707 refers to this:

> Whoever an arrow wears
> By Saint Sebastian bless'd,
> No worry has he or cares,
> Is protected from devil and pest.

Sebastian is also the patron of archers and riflemen. The medieval guilds of marksmen celebrated his feast with shooting contests and parades. In some Catholic nations he is the official patron of the infantry.

An inspiring example of devout affection is the practice, found in rural sections of central Europe, of farmers abstaining on January 20 from any kind of fruit that grows on trees, since the Saint suffered his martyrdom tied to a tree.

LITURGICAL PRAYER: *Look mercifully upon our weakness, almighty God; and since the weight of our evil deeds bears us down, may the glorious intercession of Thy holy martyrs, Fabian and Sebastian, protect us.*

Blaise (February 3) · This martyr, a Bishop in Armenia, suffered and died at the beginning of the fourth century. The legends handed down tell us that he was a physician before he became a bishop and that, while in prison, he miraculously cured a little boy who nearly died because of a fishbone in his throat.

The veneration of Saint Blaise was brought to Europe before the ninth century, and he soon became one of the most popular saints of the Middle Ages. Having been a physician, he was now invoked as a helper in sickness and pain, but especially against evils of the throat. Legends of a later date relate how shortly before his death he had asked God for the power of curing all those who would pray to him for help. "And behold, a voice answered from Heaven that his request was granted by the Lord." [64]

In medieval times many shrines existed in honor of Saint Blaise. In central Europe and in the Latin countries people still are given blessed breads (Saint Blaise sticks: *Pan bendito*) of which they eat a small piece whenever they have a sore throat. The best-known sacramental in his honor, however, is the "Blessing of Throats" with candles. It has been in use for many centuries and was adopted by the Church as one of its official blessings. The priest holds the crossed candles against the head or throat of the person and says: "Through the intercession of Saint Blaise, bishop and martyr, may the Lord free you from evils of the throat and from any other evil." In various places of Italy the priests do not use candles but touch the throats of the faithful with a wick dipped into blessed oil while they pronounce the invocation.

LITURGICAL PRAYER: *O God who grantest us joy by the annual solemnity of Saint Blaise, bishop and martyr: grant also that we may rejoice over his protection, whose birthday we celebrate.*

Agatha (February 5) · In 251 the virgin Agatha was tortured to death at Catania in Sicily because she refused to sacrifice to the pagan gods. Soon after her death, according to legend, she miraculously freed her native city from starvation and stopped an eruption of the volcano Etna. Consequently, she was venerated as a "bread saint" and a patron against fires. On her feast day people would bake "Agatha loaves" to which they attached little pieces of paper bearing her image and handwritten prayers against conflagration. These loaves were blessed in church and kept as an aid against poor harvest and hunger. The prayer leaflets would be pinned to the wall over the main door of the house, as a protection against fire.

Saint Agatha's veneration as a fire patron is especially popular in Switzerland, where even now her feast is kept as a holyday in the Catholic sections of the country, and where the "Agatha bell" is rung every evening of the year, reminding the community to invoke her intercession and help in preventing fires.

Though her main patronage was the prevention of fire, she was not expected to do the impossible. Human folly and negligence sometimes overcame her solicitous watchfulness, and fires would actually start. In such cases the gentle virgin was absolved from all further responsibilities; a male saint—Saint Florian, May 4— stood ready to cope with the emergency.

This divided responsibility between Agatha and Florian is mentioned in the following lines from an ancient mystery play of the early sixteenth century:

> If, however, good Saint Agatha has been amiss,
> And on your roof the flames already sparkle and hiss,
> Then run to help yourself, but pray to Saint Florian;
> He'll save your house and barn, the heavenly fireman.

Because the reports of Saint Agatha's martyrdom tell of her breasts being cut off during the gruesome torture, she was also widely venerated by women as a special patron in cases of breast cancer.

In Spain, Saint Agatha's Day is associated with ancient fertility customs. Groups of young men go from farm to farm singing traditional songs in honor of the Saint (who in Spain is always called *Agate Deuna:* Agatha the Godly One) and asking for God's blessing upon people, animals, and fields. They receive gifts of money or food. If such gifts are refused them, however, they add another stanza to their chant, calling down a "quick old age" on the unfriendly hosts.

LITURGICAL PRAYER: *O God, who among other miracles of Thy power hast given also to the weaker sex the victory of martyrdom, grant, we beg Thee, that we may come to Thee through the example of Saint Agatha, Virgin and Martyr, whose birthday we celebrate.*

Valentine (February 14) · On February 14, 270, this Saint, a priest, died through the persecution of Claudius II. His feast was from earliest times associated with the traditional habit of boys and girls declaring their love or choosing a "steady partner" for the following twelve months. The selection was often done, especially in France and England, by a game of chance, the boys drawing the names of their respective "Valentines." Our greeting cards on Valentine's Day are a modern form of this ancient practice.

How did the Saint become associated with this unusual lore? Various explanations have been attempted. It is said that the practice originated because people believed that on Saint Valentine's Day birds started to mate. However, such legends do not explain the custom. Besides, in central Europe the feast of Saint Agnes (January 21) has always been considered the mating day of birds, although Saint Valentine is venerated as the "patron of lovers" even there.

Another explanation is found in a medieval legend which tells how the Saint shortly before his execution wrote a kind note to the friendly daughter of his prison master, signing it "from your Valentine." This legend

147

was obviously invented to provide a belated reason for the already existing custom of the day.

There is no doubt that the historical origin of Valentine lore is based on a coincidence of dates. The pagan Romans annually celebrated a great feast on February 15 which they called *Lupercalia* in honor of the pastoral god Lupercus (an equivalent of the Greek god Pan). On the eve of the *Lupercalia,* and as part of it, young people held a celebration of their own, declaring their love for each other, proposing marriage, or choosing partners for the following year. (In the Roman republic the new year started on March 1; hence the names of the last four months: September, October, November, December, which mean, respectively, the seventh, eighth, ninth, tenth.)

This Roman youth festival with its pledge of love stood under the patronage of the goddess Juno Februata. When the Roman Empire became Christian, all worship and patronage of pagan gods naturally ceased. But the youth festival continued, as affection, love, and marriage are not the prerogative of a pagan cult only. There was but one aspect of the celebration that had to be changed: its patronage. And so, in place of the goddess Juno Februata a Christian saint now took over. He was, quite naturally, the saint whose feast day the Church celebrated on February 14—the priest and martyr Valentine.

A proof of the Roman origin of Saint Valentine's lore is the fact that in countries of Roman historical background even the smaller details, like the games of chance, the choice made for the "new year," and similar customs, were continued right into the later Middle Ages, while in other countries these details are missing and only the fact that Saint Valentine is the patron of young lovers is observed. The American custom of sending Valentine cards is unknown in countries of northern Europe. It came here from England where it had developed as a substitute for the ancient Roman "choice" of partners on February 14. This is actually what the traditional words imply: "You are my Valentine," that is, I offer you my companionship of affection and love for the next twelve months, and I am willing to consider marriage if this companionship proves satisfactory for both of us.

LITURGICAL PRAYER: *Grant, we beseech Thee, almighty God, that we may be freed from all threatening dangers through the intercession of Thy holy martyr Valentine, whose birthday we celebrate.*

Patrick (March 17) · Modern scholars place the birth of Saint Patrick in the year 385, and his death on March 17, 461. A Britannic Celt by race, and Roman citizen by nationality, he was captured by Gaels in a coastal raid and brought from his father's estate on the west coast of England to Ireland, where he served as a shepherd slave for six years. At the age of twenty-two he escaped on a boat which carried a cargo of

Irish hounds to the Continent. Arriving in France, a vast desert instead of a peaceful, inhabited country was found. The Vandals and other Germanic tribes had crossed the Rhine on New Year's night, 407, and caused a wide path of utter destruction down through France; the population, terror-stricken, had fled into the Alpine sections. After crossing this "desert" Patrick separated from his pagan companions and returned to England, for a joyful reunion with his family.

His stay at home did not last very long. Impelled by the grace of God, he left again for the Continent, to devote his life to religious vocation and sacred ministry. From his own words we know that he traveled through Gaul (France), Italy, and some of the islands of the Tyrrhenian Sea. He finally decided to attach himself to the great Bishop of Auxerre, Saint Germanus, under whose direction he studied the sacred doctrines of the faith and acquired an unusual familiarity with the Bible. He received minor orders and gradually rose to the diaconate. All that time he had in his heart the ardent wish to go back to Ireland and teach the gospel to the Gaels. His wish had been confirmed by dreams and other manifestations of God's will.

Before he achieved this goal, a great trial cleansed and sanctified him still more. In 431, when the decision was made to send a bishop to Ireland, Saint Patrick was suggested but turned down by the authorities. He was also unjustly defamed by a man who had been his friend. The choice of the bishopric for Ireland fell on Palladius, Archdeacon of Pope Celestine. Palladius went to the Gaels; Patrick stayed behind at Auxerre, still a deacon, deeply humiliated by the defamation.

However, Palladius died the following year (432), and the choice now fell on Patrick. What he had so long desired and prayed for, he obtained suddenly and unexpectedly. Without delay he was consecrated bishop (after having been ordained a priest). Some time in the spring or summer of 432 he and his companions set foot on Irish soil. For almost thirty years Patrick labored unremittingly at the conversion of the island. He baptized many thousands with his own hands, organized the hierarchy and clergy, established churches and religious communities. Toward the end of his life he founded the see of Armagh, which he held as archbishop and primate of Ireland till his death.

Contrary to some popular legends, Patrick encountered much resistance, and many vicious attempts were made to stop his work. These attacks did not come from the people but from the Druidic "priests," who actually were sorcerers, and from some of the local kings. In all these threats, dangers, calumnies, and hardships Patrick never flinched. Unerringly he went his way, fighting all obstacles with the powerful weapons of prayer, penance, heroic patience, and flaming zeal. When he died, the Church was firmly rooted in the Irish nation. In a short time his disciples completed what was left of the task of making all Ireland a flourishing province of Christianity.

Soon after his death, the inspiring figure of the great Saint was embellished with fictional and legendary details. Many of them had a true and historical basis; others, especially miracles and unusual deeds, originated in the desire for overwhelming supernatural confirmation of the Saint's work. In this the ancient Gaelic writers were not really different from those of other nations, perhaps only more fertile and imaginative. It is a difficult and wearisome task for modern scholars to separate the historical facts from fictional and legendary details, and it will take many more years before Saint Patrick's figure emerges with some degree of certitude as the "real Patrick," freed from later additions. However, much has been found already, and these historical details make the Saint so wonderfully alive, so touchingly great, that not even the wildest legends could render him more attractive.

Saint Patrick was greatly venerated from the earliest times. Among the Irish people this veneration assumed a twofold special character. First, it is not only a direct and personal devotion which they practice in their great manifestations of piety but, what is more important and valuable, a sincere imitation of the Saint. At the famous shrines of Lough Derg in Donegal and Croagh Patrick in Mayo he is not so much honored by "services" and mere prayers as by the hard and almost heroic penance the faithful perform in imitation of his own fasting, mortification, and prayers.

Secondly, in the course of centuries the veneration of Saint Patrick became identified with the patriotic and national ideals of the Irish people. Thus, March 17 is not only a religious holyday for them but, at the same time, their greatest national holiday.

Actually, of course, the Saint is venerated by other races and nations, too. In various parts of the European Continent people invoke him as a local patron, hardly aware of the fact that he is the national saint of Ireland. In Styria, Austria, for instance, he is a favored patron of the farmers and their domestic animals.

The popular Saint Patrick's celebration on March 17 consists of traditional details which are faithfully kept in Ireland and have found their way into the New World as well: attendance at Mass in the morning, a solemn parade with subsequent meeting and speeches, festive meals in the home, and an evening of entertainment (dance, concert, plays, etc.). The custom of wearing green on Saint Patrick's Day did not start until over a thousand years after the Saint's death. The charming practice of displaying the shamrock is based on a legend that the Saint taught King Oengus at Cashel the doctrine of the Holy Trinity, using a shamrock (trefoil) that he found growing there as an illustration.

It was the custom in Ireland for men to wear the shamrock on their hat. Girls wore crosses made of ribbons. "A shamrock on every hat, low and tall, and a cross on every girl's dress." [65] The merry drink taken on this day was called "Saint Patrick's poteen."

The Saint's day heralded the beginning of spring in Ireland. All livestock were driven out into the pastures to be kept in the open until the last day of October (Halloween). It still is regarded as the proper time in many sections of Ireland for the farmers to commence sowing and planting potatoes. "Saint Patrick turns the warm side of the stone uppermost" is an ancient saying. Another proverb claims that "from Saint Brigid's [February 2] to Saint Patrick's every alternate day is grand and fine; from then on, every day is fine."

So many and varied are the legends and legendary "facts" about Saint Patrick that it would take volumes to record them. The most famous ones are these: that he freed Ireland from all venomous snakes and reptiles; that he received a miraculous staff from Christ in a vision and henceforth carried it with him wherever he went; that he obtained from God the privilege of judging the Irish race at the end of time; that he lived a hundred and twenty years like Moses; that he himself was of the Irish (Gaelic) race.

The most inspiring piece of St. Patrick's lore is the beautiful prayer called "Breast Plate" (*Lorica*). It is a morning prayer in early Irish. The Book of Armagh

154

(ninth century) ascribes its authorship to the Saint. It might well be that Patrick actually composed this prayer. For many centuries now millions of faithful have used it with devotion. Here are some passages of this famous prayer in a traditional English version:

> I bind to myself today
> The strong virtue of the invocation of the Trinity:
> I believe the Trinity in the Unity,
> The Creator of the Universe . . .
> I bind to myself today
> God's Power to guide me,
> God's Might to uphold me,
> God's Wisdom to teach me,
> God's Eye to watch over me,
> God's Ear to hear me,
> God's Word to give me speech,
> God's Hand to lead me . . .
> God's host to secure me,
> Against the snares of demons,
> Against the seductions of vices,
> Against the hosts of nature,
> Against everyone who meditates injury to me . . .
> Christ with me, Christ before me,
> Christ behind me, Christ within me,
> Christ beneath me, Christ above me,
> Christ at my right, Christ at my left . . .
> Christ in the heart of everyone who thinks of me,
> Christ in the mouth of everyone who speaks to me,
> Christ in every eye that sees me . . .

LITURGICAL PRAYER: *O God, Thou didst send the Confessor and Bishop, Saint Patrick, to preach Thy glory to the gentiles, grant us through his merits and intercession to accomplish by Thy mercy what Thou commandest us to do.*

Joseph (March 19) · Up to the fifteenth century our Lord's foster father was not honored by a special feast of the Church, and people did not generally venerate him, although many ancient Fathers and writers mentioned him with reverence and high regard. It was only at the time of the Crusades that a practice of private devotion to Saint Joseph spread from the Eastern Churches into Europe. This devotion was greatly encouraged by some saints of the twelfth, thirteenth, and fourteenth centuries, especially Saint Bernard (1153), Saint Thomas Aquinas (1274), and Saint Gertrude (1310).

At the end of the fourteenth century the Franciscans, and soon afterward the Dominicans and Carmelites, introduced a Feast of Saint Joseph into their calendars. Finally, under Pope Sixtus IV an annual feast of the Saint was established on March 19 for the whole Church. It was, however, a feast of the lowest rank (*simplex*), imposing no obligation on the clergy to celebrate it. During the fifteenth and sixteenth centuries many religious orders and some national rulers, especially the Hapsburgs of Austria and Spain, appealed to the popes to raise the feast in rank and make it a prescribed holyday. Accordingly, Pope Gregory XV made it in 1621 a holyday of obligation. Pius X in 1911 rescinded the obligation of attending Mass, though it was later restored by the new Code of Canon Law in 1918.

In a short time the veneration of the Saint quickly and enthusiastically spread through all Catholic nations. Saint Teresa (1582), who had a special devotion to him, inspired the reformed Carmelites to establish a feast of the "patronage" of Saint Joseph, which was annually celebrated by the order on the third Sunday after Easter. This feast was extended in 1847 to the whole Church. In 1870 Pope Pius IX solemnly declared Saint Joseph as the official patron of the universal Church. In 1956 the feast of Saint Joseph's patronage was replaced by a feast of "Saint Joseph the Worker," to be celebrated annually on May 1.

The popular patronage of Saint Joseph is universal in scope. The words of the Egyptian Pharao, "Go to Joseph" (Gen. 41, 55), were applied to him. Filled with affection, love, and confidence, the faithful turned to him in all their temporal and spiritual needs. Every detail of his life gave rise to a special patronage. He is the patron of tradesmen and workers, of travelers and refugees, of the persecuted, of Christian families and homes, of purity and interior life, of engaged couples, of people in temporal distress (food, home, clothing, sickness, etc.), of the poor, aged, and dying.

It was a widespread custom in past centuries for

157

newly wed couples to spend the first night of matrimony (St. Joseph's Night) in abstinence and to perform some devotion in honor of Saint Joseph that he might bless their marriage. Small round breads (St. Joseph's loaves; *fritelli*) are baked and eaten in many sections of Europe on March 19 to honor the heavenly "bread father." From the seventeenth century on it was customary to have a statue of the Saint on the table during the main meal and to "serve" it generous portions which afterward were given the poor.

In northern Spain it is an ancient tradition for people to make a pilgrimage to a shrine of Saint Joseph on March 19 and there to have a special repast after the devotions. This meal consists of roast lamb, which is eaten, picnic style, outside the shrine in the afternoon (*Merienda del Cordero;* Repast of the Lamb). For this occasion the faithful who make the pilgrimage and then partake of the meal are dispensed from the law of Lenten fast.

In the region of Valencia on the east coast of Spain a strange and interesting tradition developed—the burning of fires in honor of Saint Joseph. It is said to have been started by the carpenters in past centuries, when they cleaned their workshops before March 19 and burned all the litter on the evening of their patron's feast. Today committees are established which collect and exhibit at street crossings structures made of wood by boys and men during the weeks before the feast. These structures represent houses, figures, scenes, many of them symbolic of some political event of the past year. They are admired and judged by the people, and on the eve of Saint Joseph's Day the best one receives a prize and is put aside. All the others are burned in joyful bonfires. Music, dancing, and fireworks (*traca*) are a part of this celebration in honor of Saint Joseph.

In some parts of Italy ancient nature lore rites are still performed on Saint Joseph's Day, the "burial of winter" for instance, which is done by sawing a symbolic figure (*scega vecchia*) in two. In central Europe the day is celebrated by farmers as the beginning of spring. They light candles in honor of the Saint, put little shrines with his picture in their gardens and orchards, and have their fields blessed by the priest.

LITURGICAL PRAYER: *Assist us, O Lord, we beseech Thee, by the merits of the Spouse of Thy most holy Mother, that, what of ourselves we are unable to obtain, may be granted us by his intercession.*

CHAPTER 14

Saints of Spring

George (April 23) · A native of Cappadocia in Asia Minor and a soldier in the Roman army, this Saint is reported to have died as a martyr at Lydda in Palestine during the persecutions of Diocletian, probably in the year 303. No further details are known about his life and death. There is no reason, however, to doubt his existence as some scholars have done. Pope Gelasius in 494 listed him among other martyrs "whose names are justly revered by men but whose actions are known only to God."

At an early time many legends, some of them utterly fantastic, were written about this soldier saint. In all of them he appears as the heroic and gallant knight of God who slays dragons, undertakes great journeys, converts whole kingdoms, destroys pagan temples, and success-fully puts whole armies of demons to flight.

From the ninth century on, and especially during the Crusades, the veneration of Saint George spread all through the Christian world. The Merovingian kings of the Franks (France, 486-751) had already claimed that their dynasty descended directly from the son of Saint George. King Richard I (the Lion-Hearted) of Eng-land made him the special patron of the Crusaders. This patronage was later extended to all knights, and finally to soldiers in general, and at Oxford, in 1222, a synod declared him patron of England. In 1415 his feast was raised to a holyday of obligation for Britain, and remained so for Catholics up to the end of the eighteenth century. Saint George's Day was annually celebrated all through England with great solemnity and rejoicing.

The Saint is still the official patron of the cavalry. In addition, he holds a patronage over horses and smiths, and is patron of farmers because of his name (the Greek word *georgios* means "farmer").

In the Greek Church his feast is proclaimed with unusual solemnity: "the holy and glorious great mar-tyr [*megalomartyr*] Georgios, the triumphant, the ban-ner-bearer, carrying and displaying the noble emblem which turned the enemies to flight" (meaning the Cross on his banner).

In medieval mystery plays he was represented kill-ing the dragon that ravaged the country of King Selbos

161

of Cappadocia and held the King's daughter Margaret captive. The actor playing the Saint's part had to make sure that his spear would pierce a bag filled with "blood," attached to the inside of the dragon's skin, making the red liquid flow forth copiously while the monster "died," to the great delight of the spectators.

The legendary Princess Margaret came to be identified with Saint Margaret, so the play was performed in honor of both Saints. A procession in which Saint Margaret led the "killed" dragon by a ribbon concluded the festivities, which were enacted in most countries of Europe up to the sixteenth century.

In eastern Spain plays are still performed in honor of Saint George on April 23, associating the Saint with the reconquest of the country from the Moors. These plays (*Moros y Cristianos*) have become traditional comedies in which the scenes and acting abound in startling and ludicrous anachronisms. They are performed on the eve of Saint George's Day before large and enthusiastic crowds of spectators.

In the legendary folklore of the Middle Ages, Saint George had the task of driving demons and witches away from the homes and fields. Many relics of this lore are still performed in parts of Europe. Boys crack whips on the eve of the feast in Germany and Austria, to help the Saint drive demons away. In Slovak towns and villages children wearing masks run through the streets shouting: "Rejoice because tomorrow is the feast of Saint George." In Poland the farmers light fires in their yards to frighten evil spirits away. On the morning of April 23 the dew is caught and mixed into the fodder, or the animals are driven through the dewy grass, to make them immune from attacks of demons and witches.

Saint George is depended on to watch the spring vegetation and animals up to the beginning of summer; then Saint Peter takes over. The Polish farmers have a fairy tale that Saint George lives in the moon, which the Blessed Mother gave him as a reward for his great deeds. From there he comes down on his feast day with a "key" to open the earth, and thus frees plants and flowers from the shackles of winter.

In the Alpine countries and among the Slavic nations it is customary to drive the domestic animals into their spring pastures on Saint George's Day. The farm hands blow merrily on their trumpets (*Georgiblasen*) while they march with the cattle out into the open. This inspired a similar practice for the people themselves. In Austria a traditional "spring hike" is made into the blossoming countryside on April 23. In Poland, Saint George's Day is still a full holiday in rural sections. Farmers with their families walk in procession around their fields, praying and singing.

LITURGICAL PRAYER: *O God, who givest us joy through the merits and intercession of Saint George, Thy martyr: graciously grant us by the gift of Thy grace those blessings which we implore through him.*

Florian (May 4) · Saint Florian was a Roman soldier who died for the faith in the province of Pannonia (Austria) during the persecution of Emperor Diocletian. With a heavy stone tied to his neck he was drowned in the Anis (Enns) River. Today a magnificent Augustinian abbey rises at the place of his martyrdom (Sankt Florian, Upper Austria). Pictures and statues represent him in a Roman military uniform, holding a wooden bucket out of which he pours water down upon flaming buildings.

He is the patron of fire fighters and the "heavenly fireman" who helps to extinguish conflagrations. Many European fire departments celebrate his day as an annual feast with a religious service and parade.

Apart from this patronage against fire Saint Florian is little known. Martin Luther wrote about him: ". . . Florianus whose name and life is familiar to none except that we see him pouring water into the burning house." [66] His Roman name, however, which might be translated as "flower man" gave rise to his patronage over the spring vegetation. He is invoked in times of drought during the spring months, and flower gardens are put under his special protection.

LITURGICAL PRAYER: *Grant, we beseech Thee, almighty God, that through the intercession of Saint Florian, Thy martyr, we may be freed from all adversities threatening our bodies, and may be cleansed from evil thoughts in our minds.*

Anthony of Padua (June 13) · This famous and lovable Saint was a native of Lisbon. At an early age he entered the Augustinian order and devoted himself with great zeal to the sacred studies. Ten years later, he left the Augustinians and joined the newly founded Franciscans because he was consumed with the desire of going into their "mission" among the Mohammedans in Africa. Ill-health forced him to return to Europe, where he labored as teacher, and more often as preacher, until his early death near Padua, Italy, in 1231. A year later he was canonized. He had already wrought numberless miracles both during life and after death.

A wave of popular veneration for him soon swept the countries of Europe. His life and legend inspired the faithful everywhere with confidence and devotion. What attracted them was his kindness to all and his great love for the poor, which made him a fearless advocate of the common people before the great ones of his time. What appealed to the faithful most was, however, his power of help and intercession, the result of a life of utter unselfishness, charity, zeal, and deepest familiarity with God in prayer. With Joseph he is the only male saint who is pictured holding the child Jesus in his arms—a favor granted him in a famous vision.

Many and varied are the patronages ascribed to him. During the time of the wars against the Turks the Christian land armies stood under his special protection. His help was invoked by the troops before every battle. The reason for this patronage was the conviction that the Saint, who had been forced by sickness to quit his spiritual battle against Islam, would now be glad to assist the fighters of Christianity in defending their faith and their countries against the cruel attacks of Mohammedans.

In 1668 the Spanish government, by special royal order, made the Saint a soldier of the second regiment of infantry. At every victory in which the regiment was involved, an official promotion to higher rank was given him. After two hundred years he had obtained the rank of colonel. Finally, in 1889, he shared the fate of so many other great soldiers of our times: he was accorded the rank of general and retired from active service.[67]

Another patronage of Saint Anthony's is that of the poor. The faithful soon discovered that a powerful means of obtaining his special favor was for them to give alms to the poor. The custom soon spread over Europe, and in 1890 this charity was organized under the official name "Saint Anthony's Bread," a title which may now be found on poor boxes in many churches.

In Latin countries (Portugal, Italy, Spain, France) Saint Anthony is the patron of sailors and fishermen. They place his statue in a little shrine on the ship's mast, pray to him in storms and dangers, and even "scold" him if he does not answer their petitions for help speedily enough.

In all Catholic countries Saint Anthony holds a special place in the hearts of women. They turn to him with their problems of love and espousal, happiness in married life, fertility, good and healthy children. This patronage was doubtless occasioned by his great kindness and goodness to all, and by the fact that images show him with the Holy Child held tenderly in his arms.

Girls go to his shrines to pray for a husband. They light candles before his image and drink from the fountain in the churchyard (Anthony's Well). In Spain he is called *Santo Casamentero* (the Holy Matchmaker). The Basque girls make a pilgrimage on his feast day to the town of Durango in Biscaya, where they climb a high mountain and pray there in the shrine "for a good boy." Sometimes their prayers are answered immediately; for the young Basque men have the habit of making the same journey, waiting outside the church and asking the girls to dance after their devotions.

Saint Anthony's best-known gift, however, is his power of restoring all manner of lost things. In little matters and great, he is prayed to constantly by millions of people, and like Saint Christopher, is often invoked by non-Catholics as well. There is no particular event in his life, nor any legend, that would explain the origin of this patronage. In fact, many explanations have been attempted, and most of them are quite unsatisfactory.

167

The most logical seems to be the report in an ancient Portuguese book (the event might well be historical) that a man had stolen a valuable volume of chants from a monastery. Some time afterward, when praying to Saint Anthony, he not only felt sorry for the theft but was also inspired with a great urge to return the book. He did so revealing that the Saint had made him restore the "lost" volume; whereupon people began to invoke Saint Anthony on similar occasions when something belonging to them was lost.[68] The custom of praying to the Saint for lost articles actually started in Portugal and spread from there to the rest of Europe, whence immigrants brought it with them to America.

Tuesday is devoted in a particular way to the veneration of Saint Anthony because he was buried on Tuesday, June 17, 1231. In the seventeenth century the practice began of holding weekly devotions to him; and even today, most "perpetual novenas" to Saint Anthony are held on Tuesdays.

Portugal and Italy, where the Saint was born and where he died, honor his feast day with unusual festive splendor and great devotion. In Portugal the epithet "of Padua" is never used, for to the Portuguese he remains "Anthony of Lisbon" or "of Alfama" (the district of Lisbon where he was born). There every house on June 13 displays, among other decorations, a shrine with a statue of the saint.

168

LITURGICAL PRAYER: *The solemnity of Saint Anthony, Thy Confessor, may give joy to Thy Church, O God; and let her be ever defended by this spiritual assistance, that she may merit the bliss of eternal joys.*

Vitus (June 15) · This Saint was martyred, while still a boy, under Emperor Diocletian. Later legends adorn his life with many miracles and events of unusual character. In the eighth century his relics were brought to Saint-Denis, France, and in 836 to the Abbey of Corvey in the East Frankish Kingdom (Germany). Since Corvey was a center of great missionary activity, monks there introduced the veneration of Saint Vitus to the Germanic and Slavic tribes. It soon spread all over France, Germany, England, Scandinavia, and eastern Europe. By the thirteenth century he was widely venerated in all these countries, and many churches were built in his honor (the most famous being Saint Vitus' Cathedral in Prague). His feast was celebrated as a holyday with Mass, pilgrimages, rest from work, and gay festivals.

His peculiar patronage is that of helper in epilepsy, chorea (St. Vitus's dance), and all other diseases connected with nervous shaking and muscular spasms. This is based on the medieval belief that such illnesses were caused by direct influence of the Devil. And since the Saint, according to legend, had freed Diocletian's daughter from the possession of the Evil One, he was now implored to extend the same favor to

169

the Christians, especially to the many children suffering from "Vitus's dance."

The first mention of this is found in the official *Annals of the Holy Roman Empire* (twelfth century): "Saint Vitus was a little boy; in his torture he prayed to God; whoever has the falling sickness goes to him for help; this our Lord Himself has promised him. . . ."

In the strange "epidemics" of dancing mania that swept western Europe at various times from the fourteenth to the sixteenth centuries, Saint Vitus's patronage grew to gigantic proportions. The victims of that mass hysteria were brought to his shrines and led three times around his altar or statue, to obtain relief or cure. In many places they were even encouraged to dance continuously "in honor of Saint Vitus" until they dropped from sheer exhaustion, which often cured them.

In later centuries this patronage, which originally had been restricted to "dancing" in its morbid forms, was extended to cover the real performance, and thus he also became the patron of dancers and actors.

Saint Vitus is often pictured with a chicken because it was a general custom in medieval times to offer roosters, hens, and eggs at his shrines. This tradition seems to be based on a pre-Christian practice of chicken sacrifices at the time of the summer solstice. It became associated with Saint Vitus because in those early centuries (before the Gregorian reform of the calendar) the solstice occurred in the middle of June.

LITURGICAL PRAYER: *Grant to Thy Church, we pray, O Lord, through the intercession of Thy holy Martyrs Vitus, Modestus and Crescentia, not to be proudminded, but to grow in humility which is so pleasing before Thee; shunning the things that are evil, may she with eager love practice whatever is right.*

CHAPTER 15

Saints of Summer

John the Baptist (June 24) · This Saint was highly
honored throughout the whole Church from the beginning. Proof of this is, among other things, the fact that
fifteen churches were dedicated to him in the ancient imperial city of Constantinople. Being the pre-
cursor of our Lord, he was accorded the same honor
as the first great saints of the Christian era, although
he belonged to the Old Covenant. The fact that Christ
praised him so highly (Matt. 11, 11) encouraged, of
course, a special veneration. Accordingly, we find a
regular cycle of feasts in his honor among the early
Christian churches.

It was the firm belief among the faithful that
John was freed from original sin at the moment when

172

his mother met the Blessed Virgin (Luke 1, 45). Saint Augustine mentioned this belief as a general tradition in the ancient Church. In any case, it is certain that he was "filled with the Holy Spirit even from his mother's womb" (Luke 1, 15) and, therefore, born without original sin. Accordingly, the Church celebrates his natural birth by a festival of his "nativity," assigned exactly six months before the Nativity of Christ, since John was six months older than the Lord. As soon as the feast of Christmas was established on December 25 (in the fifth century) the date of the Baptist's birth was assigned to June 24.

The question arises of why June 24, and not 25. It has often been claimed that the Church authorities wanted to "Christianize" the pagan solstice celebrations and for this reason advanced Saint John's feast as a substitute for the former pagan festival. This explanation is obviously erroneous because in those centuries the solstice took place around the middle of June due to the inaccuracy of the Julian calendar. It was only in 1582, through the Gregorian calendar reform, that the solstice fell on June 23.

The real reason why Saint John's Day falls on June 24 lies in the Roman way of counting, which proceeded backward from the Kalends (first day) of the succeeding month. Christmas was "the eighth day before the Kalends of January" (*Octavo Kalendas Januarii*). Consequently, Saint John's Nativity was put on the "eighth day before the Kalends of July." However, since June

173

has only thirty days, in our present (Germanic) way of counting, the feast falls on June 24.[69]

The Council of Agde, in 506, listed the Nativity of Saint John among the highest feasts of the year, a day on which all faithful had to attend Mass and abstain from servile work. Indeed, so great was the rank of this festival that, just as on Christmas, three Masses were celebrated, one during the vigil service, the second at dawn, the third in the morning. In 1022, a synod at Seligenstadt, Germany, prescribed a fourteen-day fast and abstinence in preparation for the Feast of the Baptist. This, however, was never accepted into universal practice by the Roman authorities.

On August 29 the death of the Saint is honored by a Feast of the "Beheading." A third festival was celebrated in the Oriental Church in honor of "Saint John's Conception" (on September 24), commemorating the fact that an angel had announced his conception. This feast, however, was not adopted by the Latin Church. The Greek Rite (on the day after Epiphany), and recently also the Latin Church (on January 13), keep a feast in memory of Saint John baptizing the Lord.

The Baptist is patron of tailors (because he made his own garments in the desert), of shepherds (because he spoke of the "Lamb of God"), and of masons (including the Freemasons, who celebrate his day as one of their great annual feasts). This patronage over masons is traced to his words:

174

Make ready the way of the Lord,
make straight all his paths.
Every valley shall be filled,
and every mountain and hill shall be brought low,
And the crooked shall be made straight,
and the rough ways smooth. (Luke 3, 4-6.)

All over Europe, from Scandinavia to Spain, and from Ireland to Russia, Saint John's Day festivities are closely associated with the ancient nature lore of the great summer festival of pre-Christian times. Fires are lighted on mountains and hilltops on the eve of his feast. These "Saint John's fires" burn brightly and quietly along the fiords of Norway, on the peaks of the Alps, on the slopes of the Pyrenees, and on the mountains of Spain (where they are called *Hogueras*). They were an ancient symbol of the warmth and light of the sun which the forefathers greeted at the beginning of summer. In many places, great celebrations are held with dances, games, and outdoor meals.

Fishermen from Brittany keep this custom even while far out at sea in the Arctic Ocean. They hoist a barrel filled with castoff clothing to the tip of the mainsail yard and set the contents on fire. All ships of the fishing fleet light up at the same time, about eight o'clock in the evening. The men gather around the mast, pray and sing. Afterward they celebrate in their quarters, and the captain gives each crew member double pay.

175

Another custom is that of lighting many small fires in the valleys and plains. People gather around, jump through the flames, and sing traditional songs in praise of the Saint or of summer. This custom is based on the pre-Christian "need fires" (*niedfyr, nodfyr*) which were believed to cleanse, cure, and immunize people from all kinds of disease, curses, and dangers. In Spain these smaller fires (*fogatas*) are lighted in the streets of towns and cities, everybody contributing some old furniture or other wood, while children jump over the flames. In Brest, France, the bonfires are replaced by lighted torches which people throw in the air. In other districts of France they cover wagon wheels with straw, then set them on fire with a blessed candle and roll them down the hill slopes.

As the first day of summer, Saint John's Day is considered in ancient folklore one of the great "charmed" festivals of the year. Hidden treasures are said to lie open in lonely places, waiting for the lucky finder. Divining rods should be cut on this day. Herbs are given unusual powers of healing which they retain if they are plucked during the night of the feast. In Germany they call these herbs *Johanneskraut* (St. John's herbs), and people bring them to church for a special blessing.

In Scandinavia and in the Slavic countries it is an ancient superstition that on Saint John's Day witches and demons are allowed to roam the earth. As at Halloween, children go the rounds and demand "treats," straw figures are thrown into the flames, and much noise is made to drive the demons away.

It should be noted, however, that in the Catholic sections of Europe the combination of the ancient festival of nature lore with the Feast of the Baptist has resulted in a tradition of dignified celebration, which has come down to our day. People gather around the fireplace, dressed in their national or local costumes, and sing their beautiful ancient songs. When the fire is lighted, one of them recites a poem that expresses the thought of the feast. Then they pray together to Saint John for his intercession that the summer may be blessed in homes, fields, and country, and finally perform some of the traditional folk dances, usually accompanied by singing and music.

LITURGICAL PRAYER: *O God who hast made this an honored day for us by the birth of Saint John: bestow upon Thy people the grace of spiritual joys, and guide the hearts of all Thy faithful into the way of eternal salvation.*

Peter and Paul (June 29) · According to ancient tradition these two Apostles were put to death by Emperor Nero (64). Peter died by crucifixion in the public circus or amphitheater at the Vatican hill; Paul was beheaded outside the city.

The special celebrations which the Christians in Rome held in honor of the "Princes of the Apostles" are known from earliest times. At the end of the fourth

177

century the faithful thronged the streets on June 29 going in pilgrimage to the Vatican (Saint Peter's) and from there to the Church of Saint Paul's "outside the walls," praying at the shrines and attending the pontifical Mass which the pope celebrated first at Saint Peter's, then at Saint Paul's.

Since the great distance between the two churches made it quite inconvenient, both for the pope and for the people, to perform the two services on the same morning, the liturgy of the feast was divided in the sixth century, and the Mass in honor of Saint Paul was henceforth celebrated on the following day. This "commemoration of Saint Paul' has remained a liturgical feast on June 30 ever since.

Both in the Eastern and Western Churches the Feast of Peter and Paul was observed as a holyday of obligation from the fifth century on. It has remained so through all the centuries since.

Saint Peter is patron of fishermen and sailors, of key makers (because he carries the keys of the Kingdom) and watchmakers (because of the cock's crowing—an ancient time signal). He used to be invoked against fever (because Christ cured his mother-in-law from fever). Above all, however, he was highly venerated from the tenth century on as the heavenly gatekeeper who guards the gates of eternity and admits or turns away souls. This power, of course, is ascribed to him in connection with the "granting of the keys" by Christ and the power of "binding and loosening."

Another "patronage" shared by Peter and Paul alike seems to be taken from the ancient Germanic mythology of the gods Thor (Donar) and Woden. These two gods had been the leaders of the Germanic group of gods, but after conversion to Christianity the people invested Peter and Paul with the function of the "deposed" gods as far as nature is concerned. Thus Peter and Paul became the "weather makers." Many legends ascribe thunder and lightning to some activity of Saint Peter in Heaven (usually bowling). When it snows, he is "shaking out his feather bed." He sends rain and sunshine, hangs out the stars at night and takes them in again in the morning. Saint Paul is invoked against lightning, storms, hail, and extreme cold. It seems that he is entrusted with the task of persuading Saint Peter to do the "right things" regarding the weather.

Saint Paul alone is venerated as patron of tentmakers and weavers (having been one himself) and of theologians (because of his profound theological writings). Both Apostles have been invoked from ancient times against the bite of poisonous snakes. If you pray very hard on Peter and Paul's Day no snake will bite you all through the year, say people in many places even today.

Various flowers and herbs are under Saint Peter's patronage, especially those with a hairy stem. The "Peter's plant" (*primula hirsuta*) is collected, dried, and kept to be used as a medicine (in tea) against snake and dog bite.

In Hungary, grains are blessed by the priest after Mass on Peter and Paul's Day. People weave crowns, crosses, and other religious symbols from straw, have them blessed, and carry them on wooden poles in procession around the church. Afterward they take them home and keep them suspended from the ceiling over the dinner table. Bread is also blessed in a special ceremony on this day in Hungary.

A moving custom is practiced in rural sections of the Alpine countries. On June 29, when the church bells ring the "Angelus" early in the morning, people step under the trees in their gardens, kneel down and say the traditional prayer the "Angel of the Lord." Having finished the prayer they bow deeply and make the sign of the cross, believing that on Saint Peter's Day the blessing of the Holy Father in Rome is carried by angels throughout the world to all who sincerely await it.

LITURGICAL PRAYER: *O God, who has sanctified this day by the martyrdom of Thy Apostles Peter and Paul, grant that Thy Church may in all things follow their precepts, as she has received from them the beginnings of her faith.*

Christopher (July 25) · Only the name of this Saint and the fact of his martyrdom are known. His veneration was widespread both in the Eastern and Western Churches in early centuries. He is supposed to have died in Palestine or Lebanon (Canaan). But very early, too, legends supplied with abundant fantasy what history could not provide, and all kinds of startling details were told about him. He was a giant of no mean proportions; it took four hundred soldiers to take him captive; for twelve hours his body was pierced with arrows until he fell to the ground, but even then he was still alive and had to be beheaded.

Later legends added many other details to the story of his life and conversion. The most familiar one is told in the thirteenth-century *Golden Legend*. Proud of his giant stature, a man, whose original name was Offerus, decided to serve only the strongest lord in the world. He entered the service of the emperor; but on seeing that the emperor was afraid of the Devil, he forthwith served the Devil. One day he saw how the Devil trembled at the sight of a crucifix, so he decided to serve Christ. A hermit told him he should carry Christian pilgrims through a deep and dangerous river. He did so. One night a little boy asked to be carried across. The giant took the little one on his shoulders and started across the churning waters. But as the child on his back grew heavier and heavier Offerus felt that he would break down under the burden. When he reached the other shore, panting and exhausted, he asked in surprise why the child was so heavy. He received the answer: "You have not only carried the whole world on your shoulders but Him who created it. I am Christ the Lord, whom you

181

serve." Then the Lord Himself took Offerus into the water, baptized him, and gave him the new name "Christophorus" (Christ-bearer). He told the Saint to ram the tree trunk that he carried as staff into the ground. Christopher did so, and the tree immediately burst forth with leaves and blossoms. The Child had disappeared, and the Saint went joyfully to persecution and death for his beloved Lord.

This beautiful legend captivated the hearts of the faithful everywhere and was the inspiration for many devotions. Saint Christopher was venerated as patron against sudden and unprovided death, especially during times of great epidemics, when people never knew in the morning whether they would still be alive that evening. They believed that by looking at his picture and saying a prayer to him in the morning they would be safe from death on that day. So they hung his picture over the door of the house, or painted it on the walls outside, to give others the benefit of it, too.

This tradition has been kept in central Europe to the present day, although its meaning has been forgotten by many. Any tourist traveling through southern Germany, Switzerland, Austria, and France will notice the large images of Saint Christopher painted on the outside of houses and churches.

Christopher is the patron of ferryboats and their crews, of pilgrims and travelers, of gardeners (because his staff burst into bloom), and of freight ships. In France all fortresses were put under his protection in centuries past. In England he was invoked against hail and lightning. Since he carried our Lord safely through the waters, he became the patron of all passenger traffic, especially in automobiles. In many countries cars are blessed on his feast day. At churches that bear his name the blessing is usually given in a more solemn way on his feast, and hundreds of automobiles line up in front of the shrine to receive the blessing for that year.

More recently Saint Christopher has also been venerated as the patron of skiing, and appropriately so. Having carried the Christ Child through the waters, he gladly protects children and grownups gliding over the snow. It was a coincidence, but perhaps somewhat providential as well, that the town in the best and most famous ski territory in Austria is named Saint Christopher (*Sankt Christoph am Arlberg*).

Finally, there are the Saint Christopher medals and plaques, which people have blessed by a priest to carry on their persons as a protection against accidents. These medals are now also put in cars and other vehicles and are popular with Christians of all faiths. The custom of using such images of the Saint started in the sixteenth century, and their original purpose was to serve as a picture for travelers to gaze on every morning and ask God to save them from sudden death that day. This custom has died out long since but the medals have remained as a token of the Saint's gener-

183

ous help and protection in modern traffic, which kills almost as many people as epidemics did in ancient times.

LITURGICAL PRAYER: *Grant us, O Lord, almighty God, as we celebrate the birthday of Saint Christopher, Thy Martyr, that through his intercession we may be strengthened in the love of Thy holy Name.*

Anne (July 26) · Saint Anne, or Ann, is not mentioned in the Bible. It was only in legendary books of the early Christian centuries that the names of Mary's parents were given as Joachim and Anne. Since the Fathers of the Church rejected the use of such legendary sources, the faithful in Europe had no feast in honor of our Lord's grandparents. In the Middle East, however, the veneration of Saint Anne can be traced back to the fourth century.

The Crusaders brought the name and legend of Saint Anne to Europe, and the famous Dominican Jacobus de Varagine (1298) printed the story in his *Golden Legend.* From that time on the popular veneration of the Saint spread into all parts of the Christian world. It was encouraged by the religious orders of the Franciscans, Dominicans, Augustinians, and Carmelites. In southern France a Feast of Saint Anne was celebrated as early as the fourteenth century. Pope Urban VI in 1378 extended it to England at the king's request. Not until 1584, however, did the feast become universal, when Pope Gregory XIII prescribed it for the whole Church.

As grandmother of Christ and mother of Mary, Saint Anne soon became the patron of married women, and for childless couples a special aid in obtaining children. According to legend she was married three times, first to Joachim, after his death to Cleophas, and finally to Salomas. This detail of the ancient story inspired young women to turn to her for help in finding a husband. After all, since she had had three husbands herself, should she not be able and willing to provide at least one bridegroom for those who trustingly appealed to her? In the languages of all European nations young women implored her:

> I beg you, holy mother Anne,
> Send me a good and loving man.

Her patronage of fertility was extended also to the soil. Thus she became a patron of rain. It is a popular saying in Italy that "rain is Saint Anne's gift"; in Germany, July rain was called "Saint Anne's dowry."

Finally, the gentle grandmother of the Lord is everywhere invoked as one of the great helpers for various needs of body and soul. Many churches have been erected to her, most of them becoming famous centers of pilgrimages. One of the best-known shrines in our part of the world is Saint Anne de Beaupré in Quebec, Canada.

185

From the eighteenth century on, Anne, which means "grace," was used more and more as a favorite name for girls. At the beginning of the nineteenth century it was the most popular girls' name in central Europe, surpassing even that of Mary. This preference was based on a famous saying of past centuries, "All Annes are beautiful." Naturally, parents wanted to assure this benefit for their baby daughters by calling them Anne or by adding Anne to a first name. Thus we have the many traditional names containing Anne or Ann (Mary Ann, Marianne, Marian, Ann Marie, Joanne, Elizabeth Ann, Lillian, Martha Ann, Louise Ann, Patricia Ann, etc.).

A hundred years ago there still remained the custom in many parts of Europe of celebrating Saint Anne's Day as a festival "of all Annes," meaning all beautiful girls. Dressed in their finery the bevy would parade through the streets with their escorts, bands would serenade them in parks and squares, balls would be held (both Johann Strausses composed "Anne Polkas" for this festival). Saint Anne's Eve was the day of receptions for debutantes at court and in private homes. Public amusements, including fireworks, entertained the crowds. The warm summer night was alive with laughter, beauty, music, and lights. And all of it was still connected in the hearts and minds of the participants with a tribute to Saint Anne whose feast day shed its radiance upon this enchanting celebration.

186

LITURGICAL PRAYER: *O God, who didst deign to confer on Saint Anne the grace to be the mother of her who was to give birth to Thy only-begotten Son: mercifully grant us, who celebrate her feast, that we may be helped by her intercession.*

CHAPTER 16

Saints of Autumn

Michael (September 29) · The name of this Archangel
means "who is like unto God?" In the Old Covenant
he is made known to us as the "great prince," the protector of the children of Israel (Dan. 12, 1). Through
the New Testament the Church continues this patronage of Michael (Apoc. 12, 7) and has always venerated
him as the guardian angel of the kingdom of Christ
on earth, as the heavenly leader in the fight against all
enemies of God. For this reason he was the special
patron of Christian soldiers fighting against pagan
armies. In the fierce battles of the imperial troops
against the heathen Magyars in Bavaria (933 and 955)
Saint Michael's help was invoked by all fighters with
prayer and song and battle cry, and the victory was
gratefully attributed to him.

His feast, originally combined with the remembrance of all angels, had been celebrated in Rome from the early centuries on September 29. The Synod of Mainz (813) introduced it into all the countries of the Carolingian Empire and prescribed its celebration as a public holiday. All through medieval times Saint Michael's Day was kept as a great religious feast (in France even up to the last century) and one of the annual holiday seasons as well. The churches of the Greek Rite keep the feast on November 8, and a second festival on September 6. In France the apparition of the Archangel at Mont-Saint-Michel is commemorated on October 16. Another apparition, on Mount Gargano in Apulia, Italy, is honored by a memorial feast in the whole Western Church on May 8.

Some scholars, ignorant of the history of religious feasts, have claimed that the Church introduced the custom of building Saint Michael's churches on hilltops in order to replace the pagan cult shrines of the god Woden with Christian sanctuaries, thus "christianizing" the ancient Woden cult. Actually, the custom came from the Eastern Church (where nobody had knowledge of the Woden cult) long before the conversion of the Germanic tribes. From the early centuries it had been a favorite practice in the Oriental Church to build Saint Michael shrines on the tops of mountains and hills.

The great Archangel is not only protector of the Christians on earth but of those in purgatory as well.

189

He assists the dying, accompanies the souls to their private judgment, brings them to purgatory, and afterward presents them to God at their entrance into Heaven. Thus he is the actual patron of the holy souls. As Satan is "ruler" in hell so Michael is the "governor" of Heaven (*Praepositus Paradisi*) according to ancient books. The Church expresses this patronage in her liturgy. In the Offertory prayer of the Requiem Masses she prays:

Sed signifer sanctus Michael repraesentet eas in lucem sanctam, quam olim Abrahae promisisti et semini eius.

Saint Michael, the banner bearer, may conduct them into the holy light which Thou hast promised to Abraham and his seed.

Saint Michael's protection over holy souls is also the reason for dedicating cemetery chapels to him. All over Europe thousands of such chapels bear his name. It was the custom in past centuries to offer a Mass every week in honor of the Archangel and in favor of the departed ones in these mortuary chapels.

Among the Basques in northern Spain, whose national patron is Saint Michael, the feast is kept with great religious and civic celebrations. An image of the Archangel is brought from the national shrine to all churches of Navarre for a short "visit" each year, to be honored and venerated by the faithful in their home towns.

The Feast of Saint Michael coincides with the ancient "quarter" celebration of the Germanic nations, held at the end of a three-month season. It was the time of the fall meeting (*Thing*) of all freemen for the purpose of making laws and sitting in court. Great markets and celebrations were held in all cities and towns. Some of this ancient lore has come down to our time: Saint Michael's parades, Michael's fairs, Michael's plays, and similar customs.

In some sections of Europe, especially in the north and in England, wine consumed on this day was called "Saint Michael's Love" (*Michelsminne*). In Denmark the drinking of Saint Michael's wine on September 29 has been preserved as a popular custom to the present day.

LITURGICAL PRAYER: *O God, who dost establish the ministry of angels and men in a wonderful order, graciously grant that Thy holy angels, who ever serve Thee in heaven, may also protect our lives on earth.*

Catherine (November 25) · She was martyred for Christ in the persecutions of Maxentius (305-312) at Alexandria in Egypt. Legends have embroidered the meager details known of this maiden with unusual deeds and happenings. She is supposed to have disputed, at the age of eighteen, with fifty great philosophers in the presence of the emperor, and brilliantly confuted them all so that they had to refrain from any

191

further questions. Upon this the enraged tyrant had her tied to a spiked wheel, but it broke as soon as the Saint's body touched it. She was then beheaded. Angels brought her body to Mount Sinai and there buried it. In the sixth century Emperor Justinian I built the famous Saint Catherine's monastery at the foot of Mount Sinai.

Her Greek name, Katharine, means "the pure one." Because of this she was widely venerated as a patron of virginity and purity. She is also patron of philosophers and universities. Since she was tied to a wheel, the wagon makers and millers chose her as a special patron of their trades. Her feast day used to be a popular holiday in medieval times, especially for students, who were free from classes on this day. In France her feast was celebrated for centuries as a religious holyday. In Paris it was custom for the *midinettes* (shopgirls) with youthful gaiety to stroll in paper caps, arms linked, along the Rue de la Paix on the evening of Saint Catherine's Day.

Ancient legends relate how from the bones of the Saint a clear, aromatic, and healing oil came flowing. This legend impelled even the Mohammedans to make pilgrimages to Mount Sinai in search of the miraculous oil. In Europe, oil was blessed by the priest in honor of the Saint and used as a sacramental against diseases, especially arthritis, asthma, and all kinds of festering sores. Saint Catherine is also invoked for any head ailments (headache, migraine, brain tumors, etc.)

192

because she had given her own head to be severed for Christ's sake.

Since the penitential season of Advent precluded external pomp and noisy celebration (organ playing in church, music and dancing afterward), Catherine's Day, the last popular holyday before Advent, became, in medieval times, a day for weddings. An ancient rhyme tells of this custom:

> On Catherine's day
> Your wedding is gay;
> But Andrew's day
> Takes the feasting away.

LITURGICAL PRAYER: *O God, Thou hast given the law to Moses on the peak of Mount Sinai, and in a miraculous way, through Thy holy angels, hast also placed there the body of Saint Catherine, Thy Virgin and Martyr: grant that through her merits and intercession we may come to the true mountain, which is Christ.*

Andrew (November 30) · This Apostle was the brother of Saint Peter and one of the first disciples of Christ (John 1, 40-42). After the Lord's Resurrection and Ascension, when the Apostles dispersed on their missionary journeys, Andrew is reported by tradition to have preached in the countries south of the Black Sea; then he came to Greece, where he was martyred for Christ under the Emperor Nero, in A.D. 60. He died on a diagonally transversed cross which the Romans sometimes used for executions, and which came to be called St. Andrew's cross.

Saint Andrew's Night is a traditional time of "oracles" for girls who pray to the Saint for a husband and wish to receive some visible assurance that their prayers have been heard. The origin of this custom is explained by the name Andrew (best translated as "manly" or "man") and by the fact that from ancient times he has been called the "most kindly of saints." Others have found the reason for this patronage in the antiphon of the Divine Office on Andrew's Day: *Concede nobis hominem justum* (Grant us a good, just man). Whichever the reason, the fact is that Saint Andrew was invoked in all countries by young women looking for a husband. Much of this lore is still practiced in Europe.

On Andrew's Night girls pour spoonfuls of molten lead or wax into cold water, and the shape of the congealing portions is supposed to reveal details of their future love and marriage. In the western sections of Austria and in other Alpine countries young men and girls fasten a very small candle into a nutshell and put these little "boats" into a trough filled with water. All other lights are then extinguished and only the tiny flames of the candles sparkle in the darkened room. By blowing against them, the nutshells are made to move across the water. When the lights of a boy and a girl collide without capsizing, it is taken as a sign that the two will fall in love and marry. In Poland girls put

194

bones from the remnants of a meal in front of the door. The girl whose bone the dog takes first will be the first one to marry.

Before going to bed on Andrew's Night girls say a prayer to the Saint asking him to show them their future husband in their dreams. Saint Andrew was always considered very kind and generous in this matter, even to the extent that he himself would procure the right man for a girl whose own efforts had not been successful. Here is such a prayer-poem from the Tirol:

> Heavenly patron, Saint Andrew dear,
> Please won't you show me a picture clear
> Of the man whom thou hast chosen for me?
> Whether he handsome or homely be,
> Or young in years, or maybe old,
> Or still and shy, or loud and bold;
> I do not mind his manner and way:
> Just make him love me, that's all I pray.

LITURGICAL PRAYER: *We humbly beseech Thy majesty, O Lord, that Saint Andrew, who was both a preacher and ruler of Thy holy Church, may also be a constant intercessor for us with Thee.*

Barbara (December 4) · According to legend, this Saint died at Nicomedia in Asia under the persecution of Maximinus in 306. Later legends relate that her own father, who had kept her prisoner in a tower, dragged her before the judge and accused her of being a Christian. At her execution a terrible storm suddenly arose, killing her father with a flash of lightning.

Her veneration was brought from the Middle East by the Crusaders. She quickly became patron of all those who are imprisoned (as she had been), of towers and fortresses (since she had been kept in a tower), and, because of the lightning flash at her death, of those whose work is connected with flashes of light, such as artillery soldiers, bellmakers, cooks, and beacon light crews. She is also the patron of architects because she was commonly pictured holding a tower building in her hand.

Her greatest and most important patronage, however, is that against sudden death (since her father was killed suddenly at her execution). In medieval times she was universally invoked with prayers and hymns to grant a peaceful and well-prepared parting from this life. Her day was a holyday in many sections of Europe. The miners chose her as their special patron because their work exposes them to constant danger of sudden death. In many countries of Europe her day still is the official feast day of the miners and the military units of artillery. In gratitude for her protection the mining town of Schwaz, in the Tirol, erected a monument to her in 1901.

There is also the attractive custom of "Saint Barbara's Branch," still practiced in some parts of Europe. On December 4 small branches are broken from fruit trees, especially cherries, and put in a pitcher of water to be kept in the kitchen or some other warm room of the house. These branches then break into bloom around Christmas Day. Many blossoms indicate great good luck; no blossoms mean very bad luck. He whose twig bursts into flower just on Christmas Day is especially blessed and is sure that he will not die during the following year. Apart from these superstitions, the Barbara Branch is now, in most places, used as the Saint's tribute to the Holy Child in the crib, for the branches are brought into blossom with the purpose of using them to decorate our Lord's manger at Christmas.

LITURGICAL PRAYER: *O God, who among other miracles of Thy power hast given also to the weaker sex the victory of martyrdom, grant, we beg Thee, that we may come to Thee through the example of Saint Barbara, Virgin and Martyr, whose birthday we celebrate.*

Lucy (December 13) · With Catherine and Barbara, Lucy or Lucia is one of the three great "girl saints." She died during the persecutions of Diocletian at Catania in Sicily, being beheaded by the sword. Her body was later brought to Constantinople and finally to Venice, where she is now resting in the Church of Santa Lucia.

Because her name means "light" she very early became the great patron saint for the "light of the body" —the eyes. All over Christianity her help was invoked against diseases of the eyes, especially in danger of blindness. This is the reason why she is often pictured with a plate in hand on which lie two eyeballs. The lighters of street lamps in past centuries had her as patron saint and made a special ceremony of their task on the eve of December 13. She also is the patron of the gondoliers in Venice, whose familiar song, "Santa Lucia," is an affectionate tribute to her.

Saint Lucy attained immense popularity in medieval times because, before the calendar reform, her feast happened to fall on the shortest day of the year. Again because of her name, many of the ancient light and fire customs of the Yuletide became associated with her day. Thus we find "Lucy candles" lighted in the homes and "Lucy fires" burned in the open. In Scandinavia before the Reformation Saint Lucy's Day was one of unusual celebration and festivity because, for the people of Sweden and Norway, she was the great "light saint" who turned the tides of their long winter and brought the light of day to renewed victory.

This is the reason why her lore has survived in the Scandinavian countries even after the Reformation and calendar reform, which brought the solstice back to December 23. In Sweden and Norway it is still a custom on December 13 for a girl in a white dress (representing the Saint), with a wreath on her head in which burning candles are placed, to awaken the family from sleep and offer a tray with coffee and cakes. The impersonation is called *Lussibrud* (Lucy bride) and her pastry is *Lussekattor.*

Another popular custom in Scandinavia on the eve of December 13 is for children to write the word *"Lussi"* on doors, fences, and walls. With the word always goes the picture of a female figure (Saint Lucy). The purpose of this practice in ancient times was to announce to the demons of winter that their reign was broken on Saint Lucy's Day, that the sun would return again and the days become longer.

"Lucy Fires" used to be burned everywhere in northern Europe on December 13. Into these bonfires people threw incense, and while the flames rose, trumpets and flutes were played to greet the changing of the sun's course. These fires were greatly valued as a powerful protection against disease, witchcraft, and dangers, and people would stand nearby and let the smoke of the incense reach them, thus obtaining the desired "protection."

After the calendar reform, when the original reason for such celebrations (the solstice) was gradually forgotten, Lucy's figure degenerated into a winter demon in many sections of Europe. In Sweden and Norway, however, the ancient meaning of the feast was essentially preserved and Lussi always remained a friendly, cheerful figure. Thus the attractive little martyr and great Saint of the Middle Ages has kept her name and her role as "light bringer" in Scandinavia, although most people today are unaware of the historical background and true meaning of this part of their folklore.

In the liturgy of the Church, Saint Lucy has held, and still holds today, the inspiring position of a saint whose very name reminds the faithful at the middle of Advent that her own "light" is only a reflection of the great "Light of the World" which is to start shining at Bethlehem on Christmas Day. It is as if she would say: "I am only a little flame in Advent showing you the way:

> Behold, the Lord will come
> And all His saints with Him,
> And on that day
> There will be a great light. Alleluia." [70]

LITURGICAL PRAYER: *Hear us, O God, our salvation, as we rejoice on the feast of Saint Lucy, Thy Virgin and Martyr, and grant us to learn the spirit of pious devotion.*

The Golden Nights (December 16-December 24) · The nine days before Christmas are kept in many places as a festive season. Since most of the religious observance was held after dark or before sunrise, people came to call this season the "Golden Nights." It is the time of the *Herbergsuchen* (Search for an Inn) in central Europe and of the *Posada* (Inn) in Mexico.[71]

In the Alpine sections it is still the custom to bring a picture of the Blessed Virgin from house to house on these nine evenings (*Frauentragen:* Carrying the

200

Virgin). Every night the family and servants gather before the image, which stands on a table between flowers and burning candles. There they pray and sing hymns in honor of Mary the Expectant Mother. After the devotion, the picture is carried by a young man to a neighboring farm. The whole family, with torches and lanterns, accompanies the image, which is devoutly received and welcomed by its new hosts in front of their house.

Meanwhile, the schoolboys carry a statue of Saint Joseph every night to one of their homes. Kneeling before it, they say prayers in honor of the Saint. On the first night, only the boy who carried the statue and the one to whose home it was brought perform this devotion. The following nights, as the picture is taken from house to house, the number of boys increases, since all youngsters who had it in their homes previously take part in the devotion. On the evening of December 24 all nine of them, accompanied by nine schoolgirls dressed in white, bring the image in procession through the town to the church, where they put it up at the Christmas crib. This custom is called *Josephstragen* (Carrying Saint Joseph).

In the early mornings of the "Golden Nights," long before sunrise, a special Mass is celebrated in many places. It is the Votive Mass of the Blessed Virgin for Advent, called "Rorate" from the first words of its text (*Rorate coeli desuper:* Dew of Heaven, shed the

201

Just one). By a special permission of Rome this Mass may be sung every morning before dawn during the nine days preceding Christmas provided the custom existed in a place from ancient times.[72] The faithful come to the Rorate Mass in large numbers, carrying their lanterns through the dark of the winter morning.

After sunset on the day of Saint Thomas the Apostle (December 21) farmers will walk through the buildings and around the farmyard, accompanied by a son or one of the farm hands. They carry incense and holy water, which they sprinkle around as they walk. Meanwhile, the rest of the family and servants are gathered in the living room reciting the rosary. This rite is to sanctify and bless the whole farm in preparation for Christmas, to keep all evil spirits away on the festive days, and to obtain God's special protection for the coming year. In some parts of central Europe ancient customs of "driving demons away" are practiced during the nights before and after Christmas (*Rauhnächte:* rough nights) with much noise, cracking of whips, ringing of hand bells, and parades of horribly masked figures.

Christmas Eve, the last one of the "Golden Nights" was the feast day of our first parents, Adam and Eve. They are commemorated as Saints in the calendars of the Eastern Churches (Greeks, Syrians, Copts). Under the influence of this Oriental practice, their veneration spread also in the West and became very popular toward the end of the first millennium of the Christian era. The Latin Church has never officially introduced their feast, though she did not prohibit their popular veneration. In many old churches of Europe their statues may still be seen among the images of saints.

Boys and girls who bore the names of Adam and Eve (they were quite popular names in past centuries) celebrated their "Name Day" with great rejoicing. In Germany the custom began in the sixteenth century of putting up a "Paradise tree" in the homes in honor of the first parents. This was a fir tree laden with apples, and from it developed our modern Christmas tree.

More significant, however, is the fact that December 24 is the Vigil of Christmas. A mood of joy and expectation pervades the life and activities of the faithful, growing in warmth as the day approaches its end. "Today you shall know that the Lord will come to save us, and tomorrow you shall see His glory." With these words the Church proclaims the spirit of the Christmas Vigil in the Introit of the Mass.

It is actually this day that ends the season of Advent and all its preparatory customs. At the same time it leads into the new and glorious cycle of Christmas festivities. Once more the faithful sing their favorite Advent hymn, the words of which are taken from the Introit of the Rorate Mass:

"Dews of Heaven, bring the Just One,
Clouds may rain Him from above!"
Thus the nations, still in darkness,
Cried for mercy, peace and love.
"Open, earth, and grow the flower
Radiant with grace and power!"—
Lift your hearts, the time is near:
Christ the Lord will soon appear.

Reference Notes

1. Saint Thomas, *Summa Theologiae,* III, q. 25, a. 5; II, 2, q. 103.
2. *Sancti Ephraem Syri Hymni et Sermones,* edited by Thomas J. Lang, Mecheln, Belgium, 1882, vol. I, p. 587 (Syrian text and Latin translation).
3. The Canon includes the Carthaginian martyrs Cyprian, Felicitas, and Perpetua. They were put on the Roman list because Carthage was the daughter church of Rome, having received the faith from there.
4. See *The Christmas Book,* pp. 117 ff.
5. See *The Easter Book,* pp. 22-23, 197 ff.
6. Council of Laodicaea, can. XXIX.
7. *Epistolae,* lib. X, ep. 96.
8. *De Solemnitate Paschali;* J. P. Migne, PG (*Patrologia Graeca*), vol. XXIII, col. 702.
9. *Commentaria in Psalmos,* Ps. XXI, v. 30, 31; PG, vol. XXIII, col. 214.
10. Tertullianus, *Liber De Oratione,* chap. XIX; J. P. Migne, PL (*Patrologia Latina*), vol. I, col. 1181 ff.
11. Council of Laodicaea, can. XXIX.
12. Heinrich Kellner, *Heortology,* London, 1908, pp. 8 ff.
13. *Codex Juris Canonici,* can. 1247 and 1249.
14. *Ibid.,* can. 1248.
15. Eusebius, *Vita Constantini,* lib. IV, chap. XIX; PG, vol. XX, col. 1166 (Greek and Latin text of the prayer).
16. For more details on these Sunday festivals see Nicolaus Nilles, S.J., *Kalendarium Manuale untriusque Ecclesiae,* Innsbruck, 1897, vol. II, *passim.*
17. *Commentarius in Libros Sententiarum,* Dist. XLV, Qu. II, art. II, qu. 1.
18. *De Baptismo,* chap. 19; PL, vol. I, col. 1222.

19. *Vita Constantini*, lib. IV, chap. 64; PG, vol. XX, col. 1220.
20. *Eis Ten Hagian Pentecosten*, hom. 2; PG, vol. VI, col. 465.
21. Council of Mainz (818), can. 36.
22. The Arabic *'uncure* actually means "origin," but in this case the term is an assimilation from the Hebrew *'asereth*, which was a name for solemn celebrations among the Jews. See Neh. 8, 18 and Joel 1, 14.
23. See description of the Easter vigil service in *The Easter Book*, pp. 131 ff.
24. The original poem had *Sine tuo numine nihil est in lumine*. The last word was later changed into *homine*, thus spoiling the rhyme and weakening the powerful meaning of the original.
25. Nilles, *Kalendarium*, vol. II, p. 405.
26. Gustav Gugitz, *Das Jahr und seine Feste*, Wien, 1949, vol. 1, p. 290.
27. See Sula Benet, *Song, Dance and Customs of Peasant Poland*, New York, n.d., p. 69.
28. The liturgical prayers given at the end of chapters are translations of the *Collect* (official Mass prayer) from the Roman Missal. Each prayer is followed by the liturgical conclusion "through Christ Our Lord. Amen," or, "through Our Lord Jesus Christ, Thy Son, Who with Thee liveth and reigneth in the unity of the Holy Spirit, God, for ever and ever. Amen."
29. Pope Alexander II, *Decretale Quonian;* Latin text in Nilles, *Kalendarium*, vol. II, p. 460.
30. Tertullianus, *De Corona*, chap. III; PL, vol. II, col. 80.
31. *Liber Sacramentorum*, chap. 103; PL, vol. LXXVIII, col. 116.
32. Gugitz, *Das Jahr und seine Feste*, vol. I, p. 298.
33. Nilles, *Kalendarium*, vol. II, p. 424 (Greek and Latin text).
34. Bull *Transiturus;* Latin text in Nilles, *Kalendarium*, vol. II, p. 469.
35. See Karl Hefele, *Konziliengeschichte*, Freiburg im Breisgau, 1890, vol. VI, p. 522.

36. Especially Pope Eugene IV (1447) in his bull *Excellentis-simus* of May 26, 1433.
37. Session XIII, *De Eucharistia*, can. 5.
38. See pictures and description of Corpus Christi flower carpets in the *National Geographic Magazine*, vol. CVII, No. 4 (April 1955), p. 491, and in James L. Monks, S.J., *Great Catholic Festivals*, New York, 1951.
39. A description of the Corpus Christi solemnity and procession in Austria may be found in Maria Trapp, *Around the Year with the Trapp Family*, New York, 1955, pp. 150 ff.
40. *Digesta Juris Romani*, p. XVIIIL, tit. 24, num. 3.
41. *Codex Juris Canonici*, can. 1247, par. 2 and can. 1278.
42. Patrick Woulfe, *Irish Names and Surnames*, Dublin, 1923, pp. 7 ff.
43. William J. Lockington, S.J., *The Soul of Ireland*, New York, 1920, p. 66.
44. P. Geyser, *Silviae quae fertur Peregrinatio*, Heidelberg, 1929, p. 60.
45. D. De Bruyne, "L'origine des processions de la Chandelieur et les Rogations," in *Revue Benedictine*, vol. XXX (1922), pp. 15 ff.
46. *Missale Romanum, In Purificatione Beatae Mariae Virginis* (February 2), English translation by the author.
47. See the poem of Robert Herrick in *The Christmas Book*, p. 174.
48. See Herbert Thurston, S.J., "Christmas and the Christian Calendar," in *American Ecclesiastical Review*, vol. XIX, p. 568.
49. Karl Young, *The Drama of the Medieval Church*, Oxford, 1933, vol. II, pp. 245 ff.
50. Gugitz, *Das Jahr und seine Feste*, vol. I, p. 147.
51. S. Joannis Damasceni, *Sermo II in Assumptione;* PG, vol. XVIC, col. 749 ff.
52. *Ibid.;* PG, vol. XVIC, col. 715, 719.
53. Gugitz, *Das Jahr und seine Feste*, vol. II, p. 73.

54. *Rituale Romanum, Benedictio Herbarum in Festo Nativitatis B. Mariae Virginis.*
55. *Rituale Romanum, Benedictio Seminum et Segetum in Festo Nativitatis B. Mariae Virginis.*
56. For text of the letter see PG, vol. I, col. 1220.
57. *Summa Theologiae,* III, q. 27, art. 2.
58. See PG, vol. I, col. 706 ff.
59. See Kellner, *Heortology,* p. 325.
60. *Liber Pontificalis,* edited by Louis Duchesne, Paris, 1884-92, vol. I, p. 417.
61. Pope Urban IV, *Decretale Si Dominum;* Nilles, *Kalendarium,* vol. I, p. 313 (Latin text).
62. *Statutum Sancti Odilonis pro Defunctis;* PL, vol. CXIIL, col. 1038.
63. James G. Fraser, *The Golden Bough,* New York, 1935, vol. I, part VII, pp. 22 ff. Fraser's work is justly famous. However, his occasional remarks about the motives and actions of ecclesiastical authorities concerning feasts reveal a lack of familiarity with the historical details of the science of heortology.
64. Metaphrastes, *Vitae Sanctorum;* PG, vol. CXVI, col. 817.
65. *The Diary of Humphrey O'Sullivan,* edited by Michael McGrath, S.J., Irish Text Society, London, 1936, part I, p. 237 (text in Gaelic).
66. Martin Luther, *Der Zehen Gepot Gottes, mit einer kurtzen Ausslegung* (1518), Weimar Editions, vol. I (1883), pp. 247 ff.
67. Gugitz, *Das Jahr und seine Feste,* vol. I, p. 301.
68. *Ibid.,* p. 302.
69. C. A. Kneller, S.J., "Heortology," in *Zeitschrift für Katholische Theologie,* vol. XXI, 1901, pp. 525 ff.
70. Roman Breviary, First Sunday of Advent, third antiphon of Lauds.
71. See *The Christmas Book,* pp. 98 ff.
72. *Decree of the Sacred Congregation of Rites,* December 10, 1718.

Index

Adam and Eve, feast of, 202-3
Advent, 13, 193
Agate Duena, 146
Agatha, Saint, 145-7
Agatha's Day, liturgical prayer, 147; in Switzerland, 145
Alexander II, Pope, 47
Alexander III, Pope, 30
Alleluia, in Corpus Christi liturgy, 58-9
All Saints' Day, 22, 121-3; change in date, 122; liturgical prayer, 123; purpose, 123
All Saints' Cake, recipe, 131
All Souls' Day, 123-34; in Austria, 133-4; in Brittany, 128-33; in central Europe, 127-8; in Hungary, 132-3; liturgical prayer, 134; in Philippines, 129; in Poland, 129-30; in South America, 128-9; superstitions, 133-4
All Souls' bread, 130
America, Corpus Christi celebration, 63-4
Andrew, Saint, 116, 193-5
Andrew of Crete, Saint, 110
Andrew's Day, liturgical prayer, 195

Andrew's Night, 194-5
Ann, Saint, *see* Anne
Anne, Saint, 184-7
Anne's Day, liturgical prayer, 187
Annunciation, 94-9; in central Europe, 98-9; in Germany, 97-8; liturgical prayer, 99; origin, 94-5; in Rome, 98; in Russia, 98
Anthony of Padua, Saint, 165-71
Anthony of Padua's Day, liturgical prayer, 169
Anthony's Bread, 166
Apocalypse, Book of, 77
Apocrypha, 16
Apostles, 77
Aquinas, *see* Thomas Aquinas, Saint
Arian heresy, 48-9
Armenia, Assumption celebration, 104
Ascension Thursday, 22
Assumption Day, 22, 100-9; in Armenia, 104; in France, 104, 107, 108; in Hungary, 103-4; in Italy, 107; liturgical prayer, 109; origin, 100-

145; for Candlemas, 93; for Catherine's Day, 193; for Christopher's Day, 184; for Corpus Christi, 64; for Florian's Day, 164; for George's Day, 163; for Immaculate Conception, 120; for John's Day, 177; for John the Evangelist's feast, 142; for Joseph's Day, 159; for Lucy's Day, 200; for Michael's Day, 191; for Nativity of Mary, 114; for Patrick's Day, 156; for Pentecost, 46; for Peter and Paul's Day, 180; for Sebastian's Day, 143; for Stephen's Day, 140; for Thanksgiving, 74; for Trinity Sunday, 53; for Valentine's Day, 149; for Vitus's Day, 171
Pre-Christian customs, 19-20
Prophets, 77

Queen of all Saints, *see* Mary

Redemption, mysteries of, 13
Requiem Mass, 125-6; Offertory prayer, 90
Resurrection of Christ, 14-15
Richard I, King of England, 161
Romanus, Saint, 110
Rome, Annunciation celebration, 98; Candlemas celebration, 91

Roosevelt, Franklin D., 72
Rorate Mass, 201-2; hymn from, 204
Russia, Annunciation celebration, 98

Sabbath, 25-6, 28
Sacred mysteries, 13
Sacrifice, Holy, *see* Eucharist
Sacris Solemnis, 59
Saint, "baptismal," 82-3; *see also* individual names
Saint Anthony's Bread, 166
"Saint Barbara's Branch," 196-7
Saint Christopher medals, 183-4
"Saint John's fires," 175
"Saint Michael's Love," 191
Saint Vitus's Dance, 169-70
Saints, Apostles, 77; Communion of, 124; feasts of, 17-19, 77-204; kinds of, 77, 79-80; martyrs, 77; naming children for, 83-5; patron, 80-2; prophets, 77; veneration of, 77-85; virgins, 77
Saint Saëns, Camille, 62
Saints' days, 77-85; of autumn, 188-204; of spring, 160-71; of summer, 172-87; of winter, 137-59
"Santa Lucia" (song), 198
Sardinia, Assumption celebration, 107-8
Sebastian, Saint, 142-3

215

.

www.ingramcontent.com/pod-product-compliance
Lightning Source LLC
LaVergne TN
LVHW011225080426
835509LV00005B/322